I0093296

Complete Couples Communication Guide

Build a Healthy Relationship by Learning Effective Communication Skills and Avoiding Communication Mistakes Most Couples Make

Mr. Ashiya & Mrs. Ashiya

© Copyright 2020 - All rights reserved.

The content contained within this book may not be reproduced, duplicated or transmitted without direct written permission from the author or the publisher.

Under no circumstances will any blame or legal responsibility be held against the publisher, or author, for any damages, reparation, or monetary loss due to the information contained within this book, either directly or indirectly.

Legal Notice:

This book is copyright protected. It is only for personal use. You cannot amend, distribute, sell, use, quote or paraphrase any part, or the content within this book, without the consent of the author or publisher.

Disclaimer Notice:

Please note the information contained within this document is for educational and entertainment purposes only. All effort has been executed to present accurate, up to date, reliable, complete information. No warranties of any kind are declared or implied. Readers acknowledge that the author is not engaged in the rendering of legal, financial, medical or professional advice. The content within this book has been derived from various sources. Please consult a licensed professional before attempting any techniques outlined in this book.

By reading this document, the reader agrees that under no circumstances is the author responsible for any losses, direct or indirect, that are incurred as a result of the use of the information contained within this document, including, but not limited to, errors, omissions, or inaccuracies.

Table of Contents

Introduction

I majored in communications at college, mostly because there wasn't a single degree dedicated to writing. In order to become a better writer, I had to sit through numerous communications classes, including political communication, interpersonal communication, cultural communication, marketing, and research.

At the time I was annoyed at the various kinds of communication I had to study over a four-year timespan, but looking back now I can see how that accumulated knowledge helped me effectively navigate an ever-changing world.

To most people, the definition of communication is very similar to what the lecturer teaches you on the very first day of class. In fact, the Merriam Webster definition is spot on. According to the definition (Anonymous, 2019) communication is "a process by which information is exchanged between individuals through a common system of symbols, signs, or behavior."

You have a sender, the actual message, and then the receiver. Those are the three basic elements involved in any kind of communication. These elements are obviously adapted according to which kind of communication one is referring to. Let's take mass communication as an example. You have the sender, which in this case would be a website, television show, or podcast (any example of mass media you can think of), the message, which would be the report, comment, or opinion piece on whatever topic, and then the receiver, which is you and millions of others like you out there.

Billions of dollars are spent on communications every year, and studies are conducted on how to effectively communicate. This is mostly done for profit, but so many of the things we've learned about communication can be implemented in everyday life as well.

The problem with communication concepts is that they're often extremely academic, and written as such. If you study communication, you'll often hear of concepts like the hypodermic needle model, groupthink, agenda-setting, adaptive structuration theory, confirmation bias, and the gratification theory. I'm getting bored just typing out just a few of the models I can remember from back then. And though I understand the definition of each of these models, I'm not going to regurgitate them back to you.

I'm not going to use my intimate knowledge of communication terms to try and impress you. The relationship we're focusing on is between you and your partner, not you and me. I will tell you that our main focus will be on interpersonal communication, which is between a small group of people. In this case, it's just you and your partner using methods like talking, expressions, gestures, body language, and modern technology.

I do want to congratulate you for choosing this book. Most people don't recognize the lack of effective communication as the downfall of their relationships, so you're already one step ahead. From my side, I promise you that I'm going to keep this as simple, friendly, easy to use, and funny as possible.

I'm going to include some of my own mistakes here to prove to you that we all get it wrong sometimes. I have a fancy piece of paper in my office that says I'm supposed to be an expert communicator, and sometimes I have no idea why my wife is angry with me.

The idea here is to choose certain communication concepts, explain them in English we can all understand, and see how they can be used to improve relationships. As you'll see by the end, most relationship communication mistakes are quite common, and you're most certainly not the only one struggling with them.

The communication process between us has already started. I'm the sender, you're the receiver and this book is my message. This puts us at a slight disadvantage because there's no way for me to communicate back to you, but we can work around this.

That's why, before we get started, I want to give you some hints on how to use this book as effectively as possible.

The fact that you're reading it means there is a question you want to be answered. Keep that question in mind throughout, and feel free to add more questions as we go along. This book will be a deep-dive into interpersonal communication, with an emphasis on relationships. At some point, you will get the answer you're looking for.

Because it's just you and me, and I have no idea who you are, you can be as honest as possible. At certain points in this book, you'll be faced with tough questions and familiar uncomfortable scenarios. As the saying goes, it takes two to tango, so your partner might not be the guilty party.

It's going to be a bitter pill to swallow. Trust me, I should know. Whenever you feel you've come across something you've been guilty of in the past, and it hits you particularly hard, walk away from it for a while. Go make a cup of tea, have a glass of wine, or just sit in silence and reflect. And if you feel like you want to scream my name at the heavens out of sheer frustration, please go ahead. I'm not going to hear you. Just don't give up.

Take notes, focus on your questions, and if I've done my job properly, you should have all your answers by the end of it.

It's also important to note that while the main focus of this book will be relationships, you'll also learn some communication tactics you can implement elsewhere in your life. You might notice certain personality types in your extended family or at work, while the section on active listening will no doubt improve how you interact with the bombardment of information each of us faces every day.

Before we delve into it, I think it's worth looking at the basic outline of effective communication, and what is required.

The first is listening with empathy, in other words, listening with an understanding of what the person you're communicating with is going through. As you'll find out in the upcoming chapters, I have some strong opinions on listening.

The second is to take responsibility for communication. One of the most common mistakes is sitting back and waiting for someone else to do the talking. If you want to be more effective at communicating, start the conversation.

With the above in mind, prepare what you're going to say. Not being clear and going off-topic are two of the biggest communication mistakes.

Expect negative reactions to what you say. If you're prepared for this, you won't be caught off guard if somebody disagrees with what you say.

Keep your ego in check at all times. As I said earlier, you might recognize some of these mistakes, because you probably made them yourselves. Don't be offended. As you shall read shortly, I constantly make mistakes myself, and I have a degree in this stuff.

With that in mind, three quick tips for keeping your ego in check.

The first step is to accept the fact that you have an ego. We all do. We all have this idea of what we project to the world, and we all have our areas of expertise. Accept that your ego will try and interfere at certain points in this book, as it's a basic self-protection method. But when you feel it coming on, allow it not to be offended. Be aware that you're learning, and there's power in that.

Don't let your ego keep you in an echo chamber. It's basically you in conversation with yourself, so it's obviously always going to be on your side. Recognize this, and accept that there may be a better way of doing things, especially when it comes to something as precious as a relationship.

Finally, let your ego accept the upside of letting go. Break down those walls that keep you from learning, and know that you will know more about yourself, the way you communicate, and about your relationship at the end of this book.

That should give your ego a nice little boost. Let's get going.

Chapter 1:

The Importance of Communication

Before we move on to meaningful communication between individuals in a relationship, it's worth looking at a broad interpretation of the concept.

As you read in the previous chapter, three things are always involved. You have the sender, message, and receiver. No matter what kind of communication you're dealing with, those three things will always be present.

The communication you most experience on a daily basis (unless you work in a call center) is called mass communication. You can easily spot it all around you. It's the radio or podcast you listen to on your morning commute, the various advertisements you see as you scroll through social media, and, if you're old school like me, the magazine you read in the bath at night.

Mass communication has a large impact on society, now more than ever. Never before in history has humanity faced such a large amount of information on a daily basis.

I mention this for two very good reasons. First, mass communication is the entry point to understanding all other kinds of communication. Secondly, the constant bombardment of information does have an impact on a relationship. At the end of the day, after staring at a screen for the whole day, you might not be in a mood to communicate any further. Or you get so caught up in social media that you forget that there's a person standing right next to you with whom you should rather be talking. We'll delve into this particular topic a bit deeper later on, but for now, I just want you to have a basic understanding of how mass communication impacts your life.

The Power of Mass Communication

To understand just how powerful mass communication is, we can use any number of examples. My personal favorite, however, is a radio broadcast that led to mass hysteria.

On Halloween evening in 1938, Orson Welles and The Mercury Theatre on the Air performed a version of H.G. Wells' famous novel, The War of the Worlds (Schwartz, 2015). Instead of reading passages from the novel, the group adapted it into a series of fake news bulletins, obviously describing the famous alien attack as described in the novel.

It was broadcast across the entire nation. Nobody had ever heard anything like it before. Nearly 90 years before "fake news" became a well-known rebuttal for anything one didn't agree with, CBS Radio caused havoc with the concept.

The reactions to these fake news bulletins offered a glimpse into what we can expect if ever an alien invasion happened. Thousands of people ran into the streets to see what was going on, while thousands more phoned the police. There were mass stampedes as people tried to get out of the areas mentioned in the broadcast. There were even reports of suicides, though they've never been confirmed.

What I can confirm is the mass hysteria and the anger that followed once people realized it was all just a hoax. Or was it? Welles never confirmed nor denied that it was a hoax, but I personally believe it wasn't.

Mercury Theatre on the Air had already been airing for 17 weeks prior to the incident, so it was an established show at that point. They had never done anything as outlandish as this particular skit, and the show had a small following, but still.

Here's my personal take on the situation. You have a controversial radio show that airs a fake alien invasion, and people start phoning the police thinking it's real. Other media houses pick up on the hype and start reporting on it as well. The mass hysteria and confusion only got worse from there.

CBS immediately called a press conference the next morning to issue an apology, but the damage was done.

Remember, we're talking about a world that had two ways of communicating with people on a large scale. They were radio and newspapers. Television sets were available at the time, but they were still extremely expensive and only available to a select few.

Now we live in an age where you carry an all-access pass to mass media in your pocket. At the time of writing, it was the presidential election and I literally received a minute-by-minute update of the figures. In addition to that, there are hundreds of opinion pieces on the topic. People arguing furiously for both candidates, and that's just one thing that happened on that particular day.

This is just a small taster to prove to you just how big a role communication plays in your life, and I bet you've never really actively thought about it before. I don't mean to insult you, as few people have actually done so. It's not just something you wake up wanting to do one day. "Today I'm going to have an in-depth think about communication and how it affects my life."

My point is that we live in the age of information overload. If Welles caused so much damage using only radio, imagine the damage the mass communication overload you receive on a daily basis does.

Speaking as a communication expert, I can tell you the biggest effect information overload has had on us as individuals. We're expected to have an opinion on everything. "I don't know," simply isn't an acceptable answer anymore, and I personally think this is heresy.

We're constantly taking in, and not taking time to process. We use the opinions of others as our own, and we're willing to defend these views to death. Not because we believe them, but rather because it's the only argument we know. The art of listening to various opinions, thinking about them, and forming your own opinion has been lost.

This brings me neatly to the most important piece of advice you will receive in this book: Learn how to listen properly.

How to Listen Properly

At this point in time, you might be thinking that you know how to listen. You listen to stuff every single day. The news, music, podcasts, friends, and your partner.

But allow me to drop a truth bomb on you. There is a big difference between listening and active listening. The latter has become a lost art, but don't take my word for it. Let me paint you a picture.

You're having a dinner party at home, and a controversial topic pops up. There's no shortage of those, as you know. A friend makes a statement you don't agree with, but while he's talking his piece, you're already forming an epic rebuttal. You want to win this debate and prove that you're on the right side.

That's the absolute worst thing you can do. While you're forming a response, you're not actively listening to what the other person is saying. You're not fully committed to the message, which you should be.

We can see this happening on social media every day. People respond simply to respond, not taking the validity of the other person's view into account. If you just took a few minutes and read or listened properly, thought about your response, and then responded, your life would be so much easier.

So, how do you listen properly? It's not as easy as just listening, because it's a lost art and one we have to learn from scratch again. The age of information overload has made us lazy to put in the effort.

Now, I could write a whole book on active listening alone, but that would be aimed at professionals in the workplace. Since this book is aimed at an interpersonal relationship, and more specifically at people within a relationship, we'll cover the basic tips you need to implement to start listening properly again.

Stick to the Basics

All you need to do is stick to basic etiquette when talking to someone. You face the person, make eye contact, and pay careful attention to what they're saying to you. This is normally the point where a person gets distracted by their own thoughts or biases, but you need to mentally beat them away until the person has finished talking.

Just this basic tactic will already have a huge impact on the way you communicate. By being respectful, and giving them your full attention, you're already in the lead so to speak. If the endgame is to win an argument, that is. For the most part, I don't believe in winners and losers in communication. The goal I want you to achieve is effective communication, which the other person will hopefully notice and reciprocate.

Don't Judge

Easier said than done, especially when it comes to controversial topics. Effective communication means you have to listen and understand where this person is coming from, even if their opinion is wildly different from your own. While they're speaking and they hit upon something you feel strongly about, resist that urge to immediately dismiss what they have to say. Some opinions are formed by exterior forces, like mass media, but in most cases, you'll find that people tend to have a certain opinion about something due to multiple factors. These include their upbringing, faith, gender, and political views.

Let me quickly put that in perspective for you by using my own life as an example. My wife and I come from completely different backgrounds. She comes from a low to middle-class, religious family. I come from an affluent, agnostic family. As you can imagine, our outlook on life differed somewhat when we first met. Neither upbringing made our opinions irrelevant, and that's what you need to keep in mind when interacting with someone.

Another tendency we have as humans, especially when we disagree with somebody, is to shut down. Your mind starts to wander and even though this person is telling you why they feel a certain way about something, and you're a million miles away. Force yourself to focus on them, and what they're trying to communicate to you.

Remember that nonverbal communication also plays a big role in interpersonal communication. A passionate person will likely make grand hand gestures while telling a story, while a bored person will sag their shoulders and look around for something more interesting. Humans are extremely sensitive to nonverbal communication, and the person you're talking to will easily pick up whether you're bored, or annoyed with them. This can do as much damage as telling them outright that their opinion is invalid, and doesn't matter.

Ask Questions

If you do manage to make it through a statement from someone else without interrupting, the natural response will still be offering up your own opinion or solution.

Don't do this immediately, as it will come across as if the other person's opinion simply doesn't matter. It is an opinion after all, and not a search for advice.

Instead, use the opportunity to listen some more. Ask questions about the things you don't fully understand or the things that don't align with your own personal worldview. Here's the tricky part, however. Don't ask a loaded question.

Let's say the conversation is about gun control, which has to count as one of the most controversial topics people discuss on a daily basis. The person you're talking to has just told you why he thinks the country doesn't need stricter gun control laws.

A loaded question would be something along the lines of "what about the thousands of innocent people that are gunned down each year?" It comes across as arrogant and shows that you're not willing to at least consider that there might be some merit to what the other person is saying.

Rather ask them how they think gun violence might be solved. It's less confrontational, and it takes you in the direction you wanted to go anyway.

The more you listen, the easier it will be to implement my final tip for active listening.

Empathy

I think empathy has been missing from the world for a long time, but I do see it making a comeback. The 2020 pandemic caused so much economic damage that it's nearly impossible not to know someone who hasn't been affected financially.

A year ago life was all about keeping up with the Jones', but now it's about keeping your head above the water. Before this pandemic a person would rather lie about struggling financially, digging themselves deeper into debt to keep up appearances, but this is no longer the case.

I used to see this behavior in my friends, who are still very much from a generation where the number of rooms your house had, and what car you drove still mattered a lot. I wish this weren't the case, but as humans, we like to quantify things. And we like to win.

I think it's this kind of pride that makes it easier to ignore the beggar at the side of the road. He obviously made poor life choices, and now he has to pay for them. Sound familiar?

Things are different now. I recently attended a birthday party with my closest friends, most of whom I haven't seen in a year due to lockdown regulations. How times have changed. Instead of bragging about our most recent acquisition, we now talk about how thankful we are for having jobs or at least having one employed person in the household. Many of my friends lost their job, and they have no qualms talking about it. They also have no issue sharing the fact that they had to get rid of the expensive German car in favor of something cheaper.

I want to say that there's no shame anymore, but that's not true. It's not that there's no more shame, there's just a lot more empathy going around these days.

Now, empathy shouldn't be confused with sympathy. Sympathy is basically feeling pity for someone going through a rough patch, or feeling the same set of emotions as someone going through the exact same thing as you are. Like two brothers mourning the death of their father.

Empathy is more complex than that. According to the Merriam-Webster dictionary, empathy is "the action of understanding, being aware of, being sensitive to, and vicariously experiencing the feelings, thoughts, and experience of another of either the past or present without having the feelings, thoughts, and experience fully communicated in an objectively explicit manner (Anonymous, 2020)".

Basically, it's the ability to share the feelings of others, without having had to experience whatever they're going through.

When we delve a little deeper, we find three kinds of empathy. Dr. Ronald E Riggio penned an article on the topic in *Psychology Today*, titled Are You Empathic? 3 Types of Empathy and What They Mean (Riggio, 2011).

The first is cognitive empathy, which is basically the ability to see something from someone else's point of view. Essentially, putting yourself in their shoes.

The second is personal distress, which is mimicking the feelings of another person. It's not a bad habit, but diving too deep can do damage. While it's good to understand the plight of someone in a bad state, and even better if you can imagine being in that same position, it doesn't do you any good to fall into a depressive state.

The third kind is an empathic concern. It's kind of a mixture of the two above, and the best way to express empathy. In addition to recognizing the other person's emotional state, you fully understand it and have the ability to express concern and support when needed.

By now you should be able to identify why I put active listening right at the beginning of this book. This, and the ability to express empathy, will already allow you to solve most of the most common mistakes couples make on a daily basis.

Chapter 2:

Types of Interpersonal Communication

We've all seen that old played-out and the sexist scenario where a man asks a woman if everything is okay, and she says it is. Then she spends the rest of the day stomping around the house, slamming doors, and sighing loud enough for the neighbors to hear.

Hate to break it to you fellas, but we do the same thing. I'll be the first to admit that I'm big into self-pity and I'll keep on sighing until I get the attention I want. My wife, on the other hand, is a master of the passive-aggressive comeback.

Why do we do these things to each other? Well, we're only human after all, which means we're fallible. We spend so much time moping, slamming, sighing, and feeling sorry for ourselves when we could be doing something more conducive to a happy relationship.

Kinds of Communication

If you Google "kinds of communication" you'll get a variety of different answers. There are top four lists, top seven lists, and even top 10 lists.

For the purposes of a relationship, I'm going to stick to five. The good news is that you already know the first one on the list: listening. I simply can't emphasize the importance of active listening enough. Listening and understanding is the first step in improving relationship communication, though each of the topics below is also worth a closer look.

To make things easier, I'm going to demonstrate the following topics with the help of an example. Let's make it a difficult one, shall we? How about two people talking about whether they should have kids? That's a topic that requires both parties to be on the exact same page. There simply is no room for a breakdown in communication, because it will end in tears.

Verbal Communication

The oldest kind of communication there is. A good old-fashioned conversation between two people. It's much easier in the workplace as you don't really have any real emotional investment. You just stick to the basic conversational etiquette, mentioned earlier in this book. Keep eye contact, listen carefully, and be respectful.

In a relationship, it's trickier, because there are emotions involved. And a history. And most likely some baggage. In other words, you have to watch what you say.

When discussing something as big as the scenario I created above, chances are you've had some time to think about it already. In other words, you know what you want to say, and you've had time to organize those thoughts.

When it's an impromptu discussion, there's not always time to think, which often leads to awkward silences. Most of the time we feel we need to fill that silence with something, and 99% of the time it's something that was best left unsaid. Awkward silences are perfectly fine, or you can give yourself some time to think by telling your partner that you just need a minute to process.

When you're talking about things that matter, you need to be clear and concise. I know of many relationships that ended on the rocks because of non-committal language. The answer to the question, "do you want to have a family one day?" will be answered by something vague like, "maybe one day I'll be ready." If you don't want kids, say it with confidence, and if you really aren't sure, say that as well. Using vague language will always come back and bite you, so make sure that you're fully committed to every word you speak.

While you're discussing the topic, take note of your partner's non-verbal communication. We'll explore non-verbal later on, but it's worth looking out for the non-verbal cues that suggest you aren't getting your message across properly. A confused expression, or a bored glance in a different direction. These are just two signs you want to look out for while communicating verbally.

Tone also matters. When we get to communication via modern technology, you'll realize just how important tone is when you don't have it in your arsenal.

I chose the example of talking about having kids exactly for this reason. It's one of the toughest discussions a couple will ever have, so when demonstrating effective communication, why not jump straight in the deep end of the pool?

During this discussion, the tone will change multiple times. The partner who wants kids will have their say, and your responses will require an understanding tone. Show compassion, recognition, and empathy. Your partner will most likely make an emotional case for having kids. "Can you imagine raising a child? All the love you'll receive…" At that point, it's probably a bad idea to use stern voice inflection to show disapproval with the statement.

But you're also on the other side of this conversation, and you want to get your arguments across as well. The arguments against having kids mostly come from a logical perspective. "They cost too much, and do we really want to bring a child into this broken world?" This is where you can use a stern inflection to demonstrate that your feelings about the topic are equally strong. It's also worth mentioning that the reasons for not wanting to have kids aren't strictly logical. There may be some emotional baggage from a broken home, in which case one will use an entirely different inflection.

At this point, I'd just like to mention that I'm neither for nor against in this discussion. It's merely an example to demonstrate the intricacies of communication, and how quickly couples can get it wrong. Especially at pivotal moments like this one.

Non-verbal

Non-verbal communication is tough. Unlike verbal communication where you say exactly what you need to say, non-verbal is open to interpretation.

Entire books have been dedicated to non-verbal communication, but the good news is that there's no need to do that here. This is only about understanding the non-verbal cues you receive from your partner.

Having said that, you can use the world at large to learn the intricacies of non-verbal communication. Just sit and watch people interact with each other, preferably in meetings. Quite often you'll be able to spot a person whose body language doesn't add up with what they're saying. Basically, they're telling you they're extremely happy with the choices made in the meeting, but with a frown on their face. It's an interesting experiment and one that will likely serve you well going forward.

But back to relationships. If you're in a long-term relationship, you should have already picked up on your partner's non-verbal cues. The subtle clues that let you know what makes them happy, angry, or sad.

I'll use my own relationship as an example. My wife has a very specific smile that is pure joy. She also stomps around the house, going to extreme lengths to avoid eye contact when she's angry. But the worst is when she doesn't extend her hand when she's sitting next to me. That's how I know I'm in real trouble.

I'm also quite easy to read. She knows I'm troubled when I'm not paying attention and staring off into the distance, in the same way, that she knows I'm at my happiest when I'm just sitting silently watching my family interact with each other.

These skills take time, however. If you're in a new relationship, it's a good idea to learn your partner's non-verbal cues. The basic emotions are easy to pick up, but it's the really meaningful stuff that's trickier. It's the difference between knowing she's angry because she's overtly frowning, and standing alone in a corner at a party because she's socially awkward. Do you know how many of those early miscommunications and fights can be avoided simply by asking a question?

This, once again, brings me back to listening. In a new relationship, you might be confused about a person's non-verbal behavior. If your partner seems quiet, ask them if they're feeling uncomfortable. There really is no harm in asking. Best case scenario, there is something wrong, and you can listen to what the problem is. If you read the situation wrong, you also learn something. Some people are just quiet when they're content, and there's no need to dig deeper.

Another common mistake people in relationships make is getting hung up on one single non-verbal sign.

To demonstrate, let's use a very basic example. Two people go out on the first date. The menus are handed to them, and one person frowns at what's on offer. It's a quick grimace, but the other person picks up on it. The rest of the night runs smoothly. The conversation is good, you hit it off and you spend the entire night walking through the city to the soundtrack of romantic indie music. Basically, you're in a romantic comedy.

Still, that grimace keeps on niggling. Here's a tip for you. When a relationship is still fresh, look at all the non-verbal gestures as a whole. If your gut tells you that everything else went perfectly that night, why obsess over one single non-verbal action. It could be something as simple as her seeing snails on the menu, and for a second remembering a bad snail-related incident from years ago.

Finally, always remember that non-verbal communication is not an exact science. Yes, it's easy to pick up the most basic emotions like happiness, and anger, but the rest takes time.

Because it's open to interpretation, you can get it wrong. There are various websites out there that supply dating advice, and what behavior to avoid when you're in a new relationship. The usual suspects are constantly making eye contact, staring, crossed arms, arms behind your back, and sweating. All of these are signs of anxiety and dishonesty.

Firstly, you're supposed to be nervous. It's the start of a new relationship. Nervous ticks are perfectly normal, and there's no scientific evidence to back up the claims that these behaviors are signs of dishonesty.

When you've been with someone long enough, you can use the small non-verbal cues to your own advantage, but at the beginning of a relationship, it's best to look at the signals as a whole, and not as singular.

Written

I met my wife in a bar while I was at college. We spoke whenever we could in person because text messages were still costly and best left for emergencies.

These days I talk to my wife more in written form than anything else.

Just think about daily life in a relationship. You share breakfast (if you're lucky), and then both of you go in a different direction for 10 hours. How strange it must have been in the old days to only know your partner was safe once they arrived home. My wife checks in on me at least three times a day to ensure that I'm awake, that I've fed myself, and that I've picked up the kids from school. In addition to the usual, you also have the odd days where you get a message asking you to quickly pop into the shops to buy some supplies.

It's a wonderful tool for communication, but there are a few problems. I'll address them one at a time.

The first and most obvious is the number of texts you send in a day. How much is too much? Is it okay to update your partner every time you get up from your cubicle to use the bathroom? The answer may shock you, because it's yes, but with a caveat.

If your texting habits align perfectly, there's no reason you shouldn't text them every time something happens. In fact, there might even be millions of people who rely on this kind of interaction to get them through another mind-numbing day at the office.

The problem is when these habits don't align. Imagine an avid texter and somebody who usually responds to a text three days later in a relationship...

Because this is the number one way we communicate in the modern world, it's really important that you know the boundaries. You'd never allow your partner to yell and swear at you in a verbal conversation. There are clear boundaries to what is and what isn't allowed, and the same is true when it comes to texting.

Let's look at a healthy scenario from both sides. I'll use my own relationship as an example.

Quite often I'll send my wife a text asking how her day is going. She'll read it, but she won't respond. I don't mind, because I know she's busy, and will most likely forget about it, but she'll fill me in on the details of her very busy day that night.

On the other side, my wife receives the message, looks at it, but puts her phone down again. She's currently busy with something that's more important than responding to a random message from her spouse. She knows I won't be offended.

Now let's look at the same scenario, but in an unhealthy relationship.

A text is sent asking the other person how their day is going, but no response is coming through. Instead of thinking of the most logical explanation for not receiving a response, their mind starts to create all sorts of unhealthy scenarios. "Perhaps they don't love me anymore. Maybe I'm not as important as I thought I was."

From the other side, the message is received. The other person is most likely busy, or not responding to the message because they're already annoyed at the number of messages coming through.

Who's at fault here? Well, both parties, actually, but let's start with the first person. It's not okay to decide for someone else when they should do something. It crosses a very basic relationship boundary.

With that out of the way, let's get to the root of this problem. It's fairly easy to surmise that this couple hasn't been honest with each other. One half craves attention during the day, while the other half isn't reliant on it, and is, in fact, annoyed by it. It borders on emotional harassment, and that's not okay.

The remedy is to have a face-to-face honest conversation about the rules of texting. Both parties can express their wants and needs, and as with most things in a relationship, there will be common ground.

Easy solutions include setting a time for texting (lunch hour), or simply agreeing to not texting during the day at all. It's perfectly okay to tell your partner that you'd rather discuss your day over dinner in person, rather than via a smartphone.

The paranoia over why someone isn't texting back stems from a much deeper problem. It's usually self-esteem, which you can try and fix by having an open and honest discussion about your relationship, but in my experience, adults who have these sorts of feelings are much better off seeking professional help. Yes, communication is part of it, but it's not the only problem.

Finally, I'd like to have to look at both the good and bad sides of having an argument over text, rather than in person.

Some people have a hard time sharing their feelings in person, preferring to rather do it from the safety of a screen. I'm guilty of this. I'll give you an example. Not that long ago, I purchased a car I've been dreaming about for roughly 20 years. I finally got to a point where I didn't have to feel guilty about using some disposable income on myself. The kids' school fees were paid, nothing had to be fixed, and all was good in the world. So, I went ahead and treated myself.

Two days later my wife drove it to an appointment to see what it was like, and she crashed it. It wasn't worth much money, but it had massive sentimental value to me. Obviously, my first reaction upon hearing the news was finding out whether she was okay. During those first 24 hours after the accident, it was just a piece of metal. My wife was safe and I was happy and thankful for that. The insurance would cover it anyway.

But as the days went on, the realization of what happened started hitting me. That car was a big milestone for me, and it was her fault it was gone. I should point out it was really her fault. She was looking at her phone at the time.

I didn't want to have the discussion in person, because I was afraid that it might get nasty and spill over to other things that are best left unsaid. But a discussion was needed because there was this black cloud hanging over the house, and neither of us wanted to be the first one to break the silence.

She was feeling guilty, and I was angry. She returned to work on Monday, and I just let her know via a text that I was indeed angry, but that she meant a great deal more to me than what was actually just a piece of metal. Why people can't simply say certain things is one of the great mysteries of humanity.

The upside of communicating this way is that you have time to think of a reasonable response. As I stated earlier, arguing in person normally digresses to topics that have nothing to do with what started the argument. The main instinct then is to hurt the other person emotionally. Put simply, we say things in the heat of the moment that should have been left unsaid.

When texting, you have to compile a response. This gives you a small amount of time to reflect on what you're sending. We also tend to stay on topic, rather than digging up old problems that have nothing to do with the discussion.

But it can also do more damage than good. When having an argument via a phone, you can simply ignore the other person. Ignoring the other person is not an effective communication method, as it does nothing more than build anger.

There is a fix for this, however. Instead of ignoring the other person, just let them know that you're taking a breather and that the discussion will continue later.

All things considered, I do think there's something to be said for written communication between couples, but I don't believe it's the best way to sort out problems in a relationship.

I'd much rather use it for different purposes, such as checking in, sending a funny meme, asking what you should have for dinner, and sexting.

Yup, folks. Sexting is perfectly fine. It has a bad reputation because there are despicable people out there who share private photos, not to mention underage minors sending each other naked photos.

Yet, between two consenting adults, it can be fun. It adds a whole new dimension to a relationship. It doesn't even have to be explicit. It can just be a nice message that reminds the other person of your sexual attraction to them.

Need more proof? In the article, Does Sexting Have Benefits for Your Relationship? (Graff, 2018), the author reveals the results of a study conducted on 352 participants.

The results are saucy, to say the least. A total of 58% of the group participated in sexting. That's a rather sizable amount of adults using modern technology to get jiggy. And while it may still be frowned upon in certain circles, it does seem as if couples are partaking regardless.

The study does mention positive and negative outcomes, but the positive outcomes are all related to people in long-term committed relationships. Half the respondents stated that it had a positive effect on both their sexual and emotional relationships with a partner. The worry and regret are significantly reduced when it's done within a long-term relationship.

It also mentions the positive effect on a relationship where one partner spends a lot of time away from home for work. The study mentions this specifically and notes that it may allow couples to feel a level of sexual closeness even though they're far apart.

I think a study about the paragraph above would be deeply interesting. Does modern technology increase or reduce the number of relationships due to cheating?

There are obviously numerous apps where you can find a casual sexual partner within minutes, but is that necessarily the option a person in a committed relationship would choose when they could just as easily have an intimate moment with their partner via a smartphone? An interesting question only you can answer.

Visual and Auditory

Visual communication is the one we most often miss or choose to ignore.

The problem is that people tend to communicate visually because what they want to say can't be said verbally. They're most likely too scared to broach the topic, or ashamed to say it outright. In many cases, the person doing the visual or auditory communication wants the other party to pick up on the hints, for whatever reason.

Let's use the becoming parents discussion as an example because it fits perfectly.

The couple in this hypothetical both agreed that they want kids. But over the last five years, they've traveled the world, set up a home, and basically just had loads of fun being young and married. But now one of them is ready for the next step. It could be both. We don't know, but that's not important.

What's important is that she wants to bring it up, but fears that the idea might be rejected outright. Why change something that's working so beautifully after all?

So instead of asking, "Hey, do you still want to have kids?" she'll leave subtle visual and auditory clues. Some subtle, some not so much.

Examples of this include leaving a magazine open in the baby section or sending videos of cute babies to him. Maybe work in a few baby memes as well. On the auditory side, she might play a song that reminds you of the time you were young and in love, discussing a future that includes kids.

These are just subtle hints to get a conversation started, but in a really healthy relationship, the other party should be able to pick up on the difference in behavior immediately.

Visuals don't just exist for this kind of purpose, for the record. It can also be something as simple as a photo, gif, or video you know your partner will love.

I'm a big fan of visual communication between couples because I believe it's not used enough, and it really doesn't take that much effort.

Chapter 3:

Common Communication Mistakes and Solutions

Time to get real, because I promise you at some point you will recognize your own behavior in this chapter. The good news is that for every common communication mistake, there is an equally easy and common solution.

The biggest solution to them all - just listen. I'm going to harp on about that for a while, in case you were wondering.

I'd like to start this chapter with one of the things that do the most damage in a relationship, speaking from a communication point of view.

Not keeping your cool, and being mean in the moment can have severe consequences. Words matter and they can do lasting irreparable damage. In my opinion, the number one common mistake is simply not keeping your cool, which leads to harmful language.

I'll give you some examples. When arguing, we tend to make sweeping statements. I'll give you an example. A man is preparing to sit down on the couch for a day of televised sports. His wife, who was expecting him to mow the lawn, marches in. "You never mow the lawn when I ask you. You are so lazy."

By making a sweeping statement, she basically just told him that he's lazy, leaving no room for him possibly being something else. Maybe he was just being lazy that day. Perhaps he mowed the lawn two weeks ago, in which case the statement is false.

In any case, it starts what will inevitably be an argument between two people on the wrong foot. One of them has already been offended, and will most likely take a defensive stance instead of listening to reason. This usually leads to yelling, which has no value whatsoever. It moves the conversation away from the actual topic and puts both parties on the defensive. Our brains are wired to go into defensive mode when we're being verbally attacked, so if you really want to achieve a grand total of nothing, go in screaming.

Instead of going straight into fight mode, it would have been smarter to make a subtle observation. "I noticed you still haven't done the lawn yet. Did you work that into your TV watching schedule today?" No damage is done, but a clear reminder that there's a job that needs to be done.

Know When to Stop Talking

This ties in with the above. There comes a point where you need to stop talking, even if you stay on topic. At a certain point, you'll say just about anything to keep being a part of the argument. You'll repeat yourself, and eventually, end up saying the first thing that pops into your mind.

Things said without a proper thought process tend to hurt, and because we know the person we're arguing with, we know exactly what to say to really get under their skin.

Let's say this particular fight between two people is about going out on a Saturday night. The one just happens to be an introvert, not in the mood for interacting with people. We're not taking sides here, remember. It's just an example to illustrate what I'm talking about.

After an exhaustive session talking about all the reasons you should go out, and all the reasons you should stay in, your filter suddenly disappears and you say something along the lines of "you'll always be the awkward outcast if you keep on behaving like this."

It may be true, but it's one of those things that's best left unsaid. These two people are a couple, after all, so we can reasonably assume that they love and accept each other, regardless of their flaws.

But because it's a known flaw, it can be used to hurt.

It's tricky to not do this to our partners. As I said, the constant talking can wear you down until you eventually reach a point where something harmful and perhaps unintended slips out.

The trick here is to take a breather when things start going in circles. When everything has been said, and you're starting to repeat yourself, table the motion. Relax for a few minutes and hope that cooler heads prevail.

Apologizing All the Time

I know this one well because I used to be guilty of it. Apologizing even though you have no reason to.

A few years ago, shortly after we had our first child, my wife decided to quit her job so that she could raise him herself. It's what she wanted more than anything, and since we could afford to live on my income alone, I wasn't too bothered. We'd save on a lot of things since my wife decided that she liked the idea of being a housewife as well.

Problem is, raising a baby is hard work. It's not sitting at home all day, rocking them slowly back and forth as they sleep silently. And in addition to that, being a housewife is a tough gig. Keeping the house clean, doing the shopping, and making dinner.

Eventually, she started resenting me, who went out every day and worked the nine to five. I used to take over baby duty as soon as I got home, but to my wife, this simply wasn't enough.

There was no easy solution to this problem. No matter how tough things got, she was adamant that she was going to raise her own kids, which meant that I had to go to work to pay for all the things we needed. At the end of the day, we were both just tired, both under the impression that we were working harder than the other one.

It was a tough time, constantly bickering about small, irrelevant things. We eventually found our rhythm, as one does with a baby, but getting there took some work.

Now, to understand my need to apologize, you first need to understand how we process anger. I'm over an argument within 15 minutes, willing to move on with life. My wife, on the other hand, likes to hold a grudge for a few days.

To keep the peace, I'd normally step up and apologize, admitting that whatever was my fault. I promised that I'd do better, even though I knew it was physically impossible for me to be in two places at once.

I should have had an honest discussion about how we were both feeling, but instead, I took the easy way out. Instead of communicating our feelings like adults, I took the knocks just so the constant bickering could stop.

It's an attractive proposition. All the guys who have dealt with a hormonal pregnant woman will know what I mean. Thing is, it's not healthy for either of you. For one, the relationship is no longer based on truth. Secondly, you're reinforcing the idea that you're always the guilty party. In essence, by constantly apologizing even though it's not necessary, you keep on rewarding bad behavior from the other side.

Giving In

I'm following up the few paragraphs about unnecessary apologizing with a more severe case of the same thing.

If you keep on apologizing, you'll eventually give up on saying how you feel. You won't allow your feelings to get in the way of a good relationship. You want to keep the peace by not speaking up.

First of all, it's a tactic that works in the short term. But I'm not advocating it at all, because I firmly believe that both parties are entitled to their feelings, and having those feelings heard.

Over the long term, the effects become more serious. Playing the lesser part leads to resentment, which inevitably leads to a massive outburst when you've finally had enough.

Always ensure that you're clear about where you stand on a topic, and never hide your own feelings to keep the peace.

Mind Reading is a Myth

This is another common mistake couples make. You expect your partner to read your mind, instead of simply telling them what it is that you need.

It goes hand-in-hand with another big couple's communication no-no, which is the silent treatment. Not only is this an immature reaction to a dispute, but it also does more harm than good. The silent treatment may feel like a nice retreat from a partner you're currently not getting on with, or it might feel like suitable punishment, but it does absolutely nothing.

All it does is force your partner to try and read your mind. This is unfair to both of you. The one receiving the silent treatment is left in the dark, feeling inadequate and powerless. The one giving the silent treatment may feel good about it, but your feelings and emotions are not being communicated properly at all.

Never forget that you are entirely entitled to feel the way that you do, and the same is true of your partner. Living in silence, hoping that the other party guesses what those emotions are is a waste of time, and only leads to resentment.

Don't Assume Too Much

In a long-standing relationship, there are certain assumptions you can make. My wife, for example, has no problem with me sending her a message saying that I'm going to the movies. I know that she won't have a problem with it.

You can't, however, buy a classic car on impulse without at least contacting your partner. "But it was an absolute steal," isn't going to go over well, especially if you spent money that could have been better utilized elsewhere. A part of me thinks that behavior like this isn't necessarily an assumption, but knowing that apologizing is easier than asking. What if she says no?

Assumptions are more relevant to new relationships. You've yet to set boundaries for said relationship, and that's where assumption can bite you. Assuming normally leads to excuses like "we never discussed whether we were exclusive. I just assumed we weren't."

Problem is, people tend to get finicky when you have boundary discussions too early in the relationship. You can't reasonably expect to be in an exclusive relationship after one date, but by date five you should at least have some idea. Perhaps even sooner if you're sleeping together.

As scary as it may seem, this is a discussion that you should have at some point, and you'll likely know what that point is. When the feelings go beyond casual to something deeper, you'll know the time has come to set some boundaries.

It's hard, but there are no downsides to having a clear, concise discussion about what your relationship is. In a best-case scenario, you both agree that the relationship is worth exploring further in an exclusive manner, and the worst-case scenario is that they don't feel the same. It will hurt at first, but at least you'll know that you're not in a healthy relationship and that it's time to move on.

Not Telling Your Partner What You Need

This piece of advice goes hand-in-hand with assumptions. Not being honest upfront can lead to uncomfortable situations down the line.

Let's take what is likely the most famous example of a dating rule: when to have sex. You might have a strict personal policy about not jumping in bed before getting to know a person extremely well, or you might not even want to have sex before you get married.

This is the kind of information you want to communicate clearly, because it is important to you, and it plays an equally important role in what you hope will be a healthy relationship.

Not divulging this information will put your partner at a disadvantage. They may not share the same religious beliefs, and will likely want to have sex at some point in time. Eventually, they'll pressure you, which will lead to conflict. See how being upfront can avoid serious arguments further down the line.

The same is true as you get older.

My parents used to be avid campers. As far back as I can remember, they'd load the SUV with tents and go camp someplace. This lasted for decades until they eventually retired. They got old, however. My mom didn't want to suggest they give up this whole camping malarky, because she thought it meant a lot to my dad. He didn't want to give it up, because he thought my mom still loved it. And so they suffered in silence with sore knees and aching backs, until my dad could take it no longer. 'From now on it doesn't count as a holiday unless it's at least four stars and someone else makes up my bed," he said. Imagine his surprise when my mom agreed immediately and enthusiastically.

Telling your partner what you need is a broad statement. It counts for basically everything you need in a relationship. Often you'll face something you haven't faced before together, and there's no clarity as to how you should react.

We can use my dad as an example again. After he died, my house was flooded by people who wanted to sympathize. I appreciated the gesture, but it's not what I needed. I process grief very quickly, and I like to do it by myself. My wife, in her infinite wisdom, didn't say anything. She just asked me what I needed. And what I needed was to be alone, but with her within an arm's length.

Relationships are tough as it is. There's no need to make them any tougher by making them a guessing game.

Not Tackling Problems Immediately

Every relationship on the planet is unique. If we accept the fact that no two people are alike due to multiple factors during the formation years, we also have to accept the fact that no two relationships are the same.

When two people come together, there are bound to be clashes. Heaven knows, we had trouble at first. And it's always small things you never think about. My family had dinner in front of the television, while my wife had dinner at a table.

All of these small differences eventually surface, and it's best to address them immediately. Both parties are allowed to state how they feel about a specific issue, and if you follow the rules of effective interpersonal communication, you should arrive at a reasonable outcome.

These also include boundary issues. I'm a friendly person by nature, which can be misinterpreted as flirting. Early on in our relationship, my wife accused me of flirting with other women right in front of her. I didn't understand it at first, because the moment I knew my wife was the one, the rest of the world became asexual to me.

The reality is that you can't tell another woman that you appreciate her dress in front of your own wife, even though it comes from a completely innocent place. Or maybe you can in your relationship. In my relationship it's taboo.

I'm glad she told me immediately because it was something I could work on to improve our relationship. I'm now more aware of how I interact with women, in case I give them the wrong impression.

Serious problems should also be tackled early on. If your boyfriend/husband is making a habit of going for a drink after work instead of coming home and it's a problem, you should address it.

The alternative to not talking about problems immediately is years of pent up rage, eventually leading to resentment. Resentment takes a lot longer to fix than a simple conversation with your partner. Think of that every time something is niggling you, but you're too afraid to start a conversation about it.

Not Making Sure You Understand

It might seem like a silly ritual to hold a debriefing session after each argument or debate, since the whole reason for having it was to express opposing views, but it's worth doing.

As I've said multiple times before, when we argue verbally, we reach a point where we either get tired or annoyed. The discussion tends to get off-topic, so you take a break. Eventually, you get back to the argument, and hopefully, it ends amicably.

Chances are, a lot was said during this argument. Some of the statements and agreements may have been lost in translation somewhere along the line.

That's why I find it best to go through the terms of agreement again, just to ensure that both parties understand the solution that was reached.

Let's use a simple example to demonstrate why this is a good idea. I want you to imagine a newlywed couple, just starting out in life. They've moved into their new place, and so they decided to have a discussion about who should do what when it comes to chores.

The trade agreements went to and fro. "I'll trade you dishwashing duty for cleaning the bathroom," and so forth. Eventually, an agreement was reached, but it wasn't scribbled down on paper and there was no debrief.

A few days later the wife arrives home, wondering why the dishes are piled to the roof. The man responds by stating that he thought he traded that horrible chore for cleaning the bathroom.

It's a silly, simple example, but it demonstrates how parts of discussions are often overlooked. My advice is to just run through whatever you talked about again, just to ensure you're both on the same page.

Dismissing Dreams, Fears and Ideas

Not taking your partner's dreams, fears and ideas seriously is more a form of manipulation than anything else, but there is a connection to communication.

In a healthy relationship, dreams, fears, and ideas are some of the main things you should be sharing with your partner. It's how you progress through life and decide what the end goal is going to be. All our biggest achievements stem from these three things.

Dismissing them is basically a way of saying that your partner's ambitions and fears don't matter. You may be a victim of this kind of abuse yourself. And yes, I do consider emotional manipulation abuse, because of the emotional impact it has.

When done long enough, the person whose ideas and fears are constantly dismissed start to doubt themselves.

They're less inclined to speak up, and more likely to submit to the wishes of their partner. That's why I call it manipulation.

Self-doubt stands in the way of effective communication. The person will start to wonder whether their emotions, opinions, and comments even matter. You can see how this creates a massive problem. Effectively, you only have one person in charge of the relationship, making all the big decisions.

My advice here is to recognize when your dreams, fears and ideas are constantly being dismissed, and to not let it get you down. As one half of a relationship, you deserve to be heard loud and clear.

Be Willing to Repair

The fact that you're reading this is already proof that you're on the right path. You've recognized that there are communication problems in your relationship, and you want to repair them.

Quite often it's easier to walk away from a relationship, rather than trying to fix it. It's not such a big deal when the relationship is fresh, but it cuts a bit deeper when two people who have been together for decades decide to call it quits.

The sad thing is that communication in a relationship isn't that hard. We haven't covered anything that's even remotely hard so far. The trick to effective communication in a relationship is to be mindful and to recognize all the traps. All of them are right here in this book, but you have to be willing to put in the work to repair it.

As I said, to most people it just seems easier to walk away, which is one of the most common communication mistakes. There's this existing idea that communication is hard, but it just isn't.

Not Listening

This chapter was always going to end with a reminder to listen properly. Don't formulate your counter-argument while your partner is speaking. Listen to what they have to say, and then only think about your response.

Here's the ultimate tip for really listening to a person. Forget about your side of the argument for a few minutes, and put yourself in their shoes. Look at it from their side.

I want to use a real-life example that has been bothering me for years. My wife is still best friends with the first person she met on the first day of school. They've been through a lot together, and they tend to share their victories, woes and everything in between with each other.

She has a problem with her husband. He never wanted kids, yet they decided to get married anyway. She always hoped that she could wear him down until he accepted, which he eventually did.

Now she's struggling to get him to interact with his son. A normal afternoon for him is coming home, retreating to his man cave for a gaming session, and going to bed when he's tired. He makes no contribution to raising his child, other than the financial obligations.

This obviously has a drastic effect on the woman's life. She also has a full-time job and commitments. Once those commitments are finished for the day, she has to go home, make dinner, feed the child, bathe the child, and then put him to bed. While all of this is happening, her husband is blissfully gaming away in his mancave.

Naturally, there have been arguments. I discussed the art of listening earlier in this book, so I won't go any deeper into that. You can go back to chapter one and decide for yourself how active listening is applicable to this situation.

What I want to explore here is imagining what life must be like for the other person.

The husband needs to sit down and go through his wife's daily routine. Not just thinking about it, but also the effects it has on her body and mind. After a day at work, one is usually tired. Imagine how emotionally draining it must be knowing that you still have all that work to do once you get home. If he really commits to putting himself in her shoes, there can only be one logical conclusion. Perhaps his time spent gaming would be better spent bonding with his son, or, at the very least, helping out around the house so his wife can take a breather.

It takes two to tango, however. The goal of this exercise is not to vilify the husband, but to look at both sides of the story objectively. So let's take a gander at the husband's life and the possible emotions connected to it.

The first thing we need to take into account is that he never wanted kids. He eventually relented and did it anyway, which could possibly mean there may be some resentment towards his wife and the child? Either way, one could argue it was a poor life choice and one that they are both guilty of.

This resentment eventually builds to a point where he no longer feels at home in his own home. It's a mess, there are constant noises and a child running around. It's not what he signed up for when he married his wife, so he retreats to his own safe space to get away from it all.

I'll leave it up for you to decide whose side you're on. The main objective here was to look at a story from both sides, and how difficult it is. Your immediate reaction is to vilify the husband, but that means completely ignoring his feelings.

As tough as it may be, try and implement this tactic in your own life. Whenever you get stuck in a messy argument or differing opinions on a big life decision, take a step back and look at the situation through the eyes of your partner. I promise you that you'll get some sense of clarity, or at least some insight that will lead you to ask questions to understand their position a bit better.

The Results of These Mistakes

The most common result is misunderstandings. A lack of proper communication in a relationship, be it verbal or non-verbal, will lead to misunderstandings, which will lead to a whole host of problems. The most common one I can think of is not having clear relationship boundaries, especially when the relationship is new. When I look at my own life, I can also see that I still make the mistake of not listening properly. My wife will often talk to me while my mind is a million miles away. Then, when Sunday arrives and a whole host of people arrive at my house and I wonder why, I realize that's what she was talking about when I wasn't listening.

The second common result is unnecessary conflict. My example above is the perfect example. I'll ask my wife what all these people are doing here, and she'll say that she told me days ago. Suddenly I'm not just caught off guard by visitors, but my wife also knows that I wasn't paying attention. This really annoys her, and I can almost guarantee that I'm going to receive a stern talking to later on.

If you don't communicate properly within your relationship, you might learn things about it via the grapevine. Instead of telling your partner that you're finally ready to have the discussion about whether to have kids or not, you decide to rather have it with a good friend. The next time all of you get together, this friend's husband asks you whether you made a decision about having kids yet. You have no idea what he's talking about, but it's clear that discussions have been going on behind your back.

This leads to mistrust, which is a relationship killer.

But fear not, for we shall look at remedies for these problems soon enough.

Chapter 4:

Fundamental Relationship Needs

The Requirements of a Healthy Relationship

As I mentioned earlier in this book, no two relationships are the same, because no two people are the same. I have no idea what your relationship is like, and what your deepest desires are. We can, however, work according to the basic needs of every human. Just like we need oxygen, food, and water to sustain our bodies, we need certain things to keep our minds intact.

In the book Relationship Breakthrough (Madanes, 2013), the author gives us six basic relationship needs. I reckon we can take it a few steps further than that, but for now, we'll just focus on these.

Reliability and Safety

Think about where you're sitting right now. Do you feel safe? Why do you feel safe? Why are you content?

Chances are you're sitting comfortably in a chair at home, which you have enough money to pay for month to month. You already had dinner, and maybe you're enjoying a glass of wine while you read this. The doors are locked, the neighborhood is quiet and the police are five minutes away. You're safe, secure, and fed. Those are just some of your basic needs as a human.

Reliability and safety are also important in a relationship. You want to know that you can rely on your partner for whatever. Safety doesn't necessarily mean protection from intruders, but rather a state of mind. You feel safe around them like you can tell them anything without fear of judgment.

Already we can see how this fits in with relationship communication. If you don't have the freedom to communicate openly with your partner, a big chunk of a healthy relationship isn't present. Reliability also plays a huge role. Most of us take comfort in the fact that we have someone at home who will listen to our gripes, no matter how small they are.

My wife likes to vent every night after the kids have gone to bed. She'll spend five minutes telling me about her day, complaining about the various things one faces on any given day. Like traffic, or annoying co-workers.

Variety

This may be in stark contrast to what I wrote above, but we all do like a bit of variety. Why else do we go away on holidays? To get away from our normal routines and to experience something else for a change.

Variety is more important in a relationship than you might think. While contentment is a good thing, we should always ensure that we step outside our comfort zones every once in a while.

I'll give you an example of how routine can damage a relationship. Most of us know it as empty nest syndrome, and it has a nasty habit of leading to divorce. To understand why, we need to look at life while kids were in the house, and life after.

While the kids were there, the parent in charge of ferrying them around had a life based around those kids. They'd drive them to school, help with projects, go shopping for new clothes and other necessities, as well as hand out advice. It's worth stating that the other parent also plays a huge role, if only in the evenings, and over weekends.

Remove the kids and suddenly you have this massive void, especially for the parent on who the kids relied the most on a day-to-day basis. But it's not just the void that's the problem. In today's fast-paced world, we tend to live past one another. The family arrives at home, everyone has dinner, maybe you all watch some television together, and then it's off to bed.

Eventually, you and your partner live past one another. You never get time to talk, because there's always something going on with the kids. The weekly routine, not to mention birthday parties, or activities over the weekend.

Once the kids are away, you're left in a big empty house with a person you no longer know, all because you never took the time to add some variety to life. You went all those years without taking a breather, never taking the time to catch up or talk to your significant other. It also doesn't help that people change over time, and if you don't take the time to talk and grow with the other person, they will be a stranger to you.

People are always surprised when I tell them my wife is the most important thing in my life, and the relationship I work the hardest on. "You have a child," they say. "How could he possibly not be the most important thing in your life?"

Thing is, at a certain point he'll leave the house, and start his own life. At that point I'll only be 50 years old, hopefully with a few good years still left over. I love my child, but I make a point of constantly nurturing my relationship with my wife. We have a lifetime to spend together, while our son will only be a constant part of that lifetime for maybe 20 years.

Feeling Wanted

I don't know of a single person who doesn't want to feel wanted, or significant.

There are upsides and downsides to this. Significance is unfortunately often quantified by the amount of success you achieve. There is a sort of success hierarchy where a lawyer is more significant than a burger flipper.

This is a cultural thing. I remember visiting Basel in Switzerland a few years ago. While I was having an overpriced pretentious cappuccino, the street sweeper arrived on the other side of the street. Normally people would go out of their way to avoid somebody with such a seemingly lowly job, but the people of Switzerland greeted him as friendly as they greeted people wearing suits. Even more impressive than that, you could see that he enjoyed his job. He took great care of the streets and even checked the trees on the side of the road to see if they were fine. I learned a valuable lesson that day. We should never judge people by the job that they do. Not just because every tiny job, no matter how insignificant contributes to the economy, but because a person is more than just their job.

In addition to feeling significant in their jobs, or whatever other parts of life a person deems important (like fatherhood), a person also wants to feel significant in a relationship.

This is particularly hard in the modern world, where traditional gender roles no longer apply. In our household, I'm in charge of raising the child after my wife decided to go back to a life of making television after spending the initial six years at home. I clean, cook, do the school run, and help with homework.

Some men would feel insignificant given the job, but it gives me great joy to take care of the child and the house. My wife takes great joy in bringing home the bacon, as well as once again doing the job she studied so hard to do.

But the significance isn't just tied to the jobs we do. In a relationship, it's tied to how we treat each other. In an earlier chapter, I wrote about dismissing somebody's hopes, dreams, and fears, as well as apologizing too much. Both these things lead to resentment, and the root of that resentment is the feeling that you don't matter as much.

Connection

This one isn't hard to explain. It's basically being in touch with the ones you love, which includes your romantic partner. You feel comfortable sharing your feelings, and you feel important. You feel loved, warm, and safe.

There are also connections on a deeper level. Some couples have the ability to talk without even speaking a word. On many occasions, something odd will happen, or some controversial statement will be made at a party and I'll look at my wife. She'll look right back, and without exchanging a word, she'll already know what I'm thinking at that point in time.

You also have some connections shared via grief. I'll give you a personal example. My wife lost her father to cancer shortly after we started dating. It was a tough ride, but it was one of those things that made me even more certain that she was the woman I wanted to spend my life with.

Ten years later my own dad died of a heart attack. Until then, I had no point of reference for what my wife lost.

She, on the other hand, knew exactly what I was going through and what I needed.

It may seem a bit somber, but us both being a part of the Dead Dad club brought us together even closer. We connected once again on a whole new level, now both understanding what proper loss is.

Growth

Growth takes its place on top of Maslow's hierarchy of needs. In case you're now familiar with the concept, Abraham Maslow published a study in 1943 titled, A Theory of Human Motivation (Maslow, 1943). It has become the gold standard for understanding basic human needs, no matter race, religion, culture, or age.

The pyramid starts with the most basic need, which is obviously physiological - oxygen, food, and water. The second tier is safety, the third loving, and belonging, and the fourth is esteem. Right on top of all of this is growth.

Essentially, this means we need to constantly grow as individuals on multiple levels - spiritually, intellectually, and emotionally. Just think about yourself for a second. Are you the same person you were when you were 21? I'm most definitely not. I was wearing nu-metal shirts, rebelling against capitalism and the man. I'm almost 100% sure that you've also come to the realization that certain things are in place because they work. We also grow emotionally as we experience joy and trauma (a child's birth, or the death of a loved one), and we grow spiritually as we learn to appreciate the more important things in life.

Growth in a relationship is just as important as individual growth. As you progress through life, your goals change. So does your metric for success. When you're young and just married, you want to travel the world. Once you have kids, you put away every extra cent towards their college fund.

A very simple example is sex. When you're a newlywed, there's a lot of it. When you've been married for more than 10 years? Not so much. While sexual health is good, it's also good to replace that initial sexual attraction with another kind of intimacy.

Naturally, growth is also key in communication between couples. By reading this book, you're currently growing.

Contribution

This isn't about wanting your partner to contribute to your relationship, but rather about you wanting to contribute to the world at large. According to Relationship Breakthrough (Madenes, 2013), a contribution is a great way to modulate the five other needs mentioned in this list. Once you feel the need to contribute to the world, and, more importantly, more than what is expected in your relationship, it means everything else in this list is in place.

It shows great personal growth, for example. It demonstrates a deeper connection with yourself, the world and your spouse. You feel significant because of your contributions, but that's not why you do it. (See, once again some growth.) And, naturally, there's variety in contributing because it interrupts your everyday life.

Most importantly, it shows that you feel safe in your life in general, and in your relationship. Once you start giving back, you've reached a Nirvana relationship.

Some Other Needs

The six needs mentioned above are extremely broad. They're applicable to an interpersonal relationship, but also to the world around you in general. When it comes to the needs of just two people, the list is a bit simpler. You might even call it a bit selfish, and somewhat picky, but since these recommendations were written by someone with a doctorate in psychology, I think we should take them seriously.

In an article called 10 Things Your Relationship Needs to Thrive, Barton Goldsmith Ph.D. makes some compelling arguments (Goldsmith, 2013).

He starts off by stating what should be obvious to you by now. The first requirements are constant communication and kindness, as well as the tenacity to work through troubled times. Since we've already covered both, we'll move on to the rest.

According to Goldsmith, a sense of humor is also a must. It's not something we think about often, but a person's ability to make us laugh or feel good ranks rather high on the list of must-haves we look for in a partner. And not just initially either. As you grow older, you realize that certain things aren't as important as they once were, and you'll laugh at how ignorant you once were. More than that, you have to have the ability to laugh at yourself and laugh at insignificant arguments you may have had over the years.

The next tip is to share life lessons. As I mentioned earlier, my wife and I come from very different religious backgrounds. Not having any experience with religion, I was fascinated by the concept of blind faith. So, one day I asked my wife why she believes, and she responded with words I'll never forget. "Because it's harder than not believing." That's a life lesson about religion right there.

The idea behind it is to constantly learn from each other. I used to suffer from severe road rage, having been stuck in traffic for more than three hours each day. Until one day I came to the realization that swearing and making rude gestures behind the wheel is absolutely meaningless. All it does is elevate your blood pressure and anxiety levels until you eventually arrive home in an aggravated state. I tried blissful ignorance instead, and I've never looked back. I just sit there, listening to the soothing sounds of my favorite music, watching the chaos play out in front of me. I shared this with my wife, and it worked for her as well.

Compliments

It's a small form of verbal communication, but it works wonders. You'd be surprised at how you can brighten your partner's day simply by telling them that they look beautiful. You can also do it by sending a message as mentioned earlier. A small gesture like this goes a long way toward making someone feel special, loved, and wanted.

Romance and Sex

It's a pity that both romance and sex tend to fizzle out as a relationship grows older. There are many contributing factors.

The number one killer of sex and romance is kids. Once the kids are put to bed, you're likely so exhausted that you're not really in the mood. Even if you force yourself to partake, it's not exactly romantic or intimate, is it?

You may also have a disinterest in your partner, stemming from a fear of underperforming or perhaps even body image.

At a certain point, you may even ask yourself if sex is even that important, and I'm here to tell you that it most definitely is. In addition to all that feel-good hormones it releases, it also relieves stress, boosts confidence, and it's the ultimate act of intimacy. The more sex you have, the more this intimacy will spill into the rest of your life.

And let's not forget how well you sleep after you've done the deed…

Admitting Mistakes and Forgiveness

It's an inevitable part of existence that you will make a mess of things at some point, especially when it comes to relationships. The tricky bit is admitting these mistakes and asking forgiveness for them.

It is necessary, however. If you don't fess up to a mistake and apologize for it, you run the risk of your partner no longer trusting you as they did before. Whatever it was that you did will become expected, part of the new normal in your relationship. Leaving things unsaid is like a festering wound, as I mentioned before. It doesn't do as much damage right away, but over time it leads to resentment.

This isn't just about admitting your mistakes to your partner and asking for their forgiveness. You have to do the same for yourself, or you'll end up resenting yourself. Not doing this usually leads to regret, which is a useless emotion.

Chapter 5:

Common Relationship Mistakes

From what you've read so far, it's fairly obvious that the most common relationship mistake is a lack or a breakdown of communication.

So far I've only given hints, suggestions, and some light advice on how to improve communication in your relationship. We started with the basics of communication, moved on to common communication mistakes, and also the most fundamental communication needs.

In this chapter we'll look at the most common mistakes we make in a relationship, as well as how to solve them with communication. These hints will be short and sweet, as the next chapter in this book will be dedicated solely to improving your skills as a communicator. Naturally, these will be applicable to your relationship, but as an added bonus you can also apply them to almost every other relationship you have, whether it be family or close friends.

For now, here are the biggest and most common relationship stumbling blocks new and old couples face, starting with the more serious stuff, and moving on to the lesser mistakes as we move on.

The first nine mistakes are based on a *Psychology Today* article penned by the psychologist, Susan Krauss Whitbourne Ph.D. It's called The 9 Most Common Relationship Mistakes (Whitbourne, 2014) and it explicitly mentions that these are the nine most likely suspects to sink a relationship.

Taking a Partner for Granted

Taking your partner for granted is an easy mistake to make because it's not something you actively do. It's the kind of behavior that comes over a long period of time.

I'm not talking about the everyday nice things you do for each other, like making the bed, bringing flowers home, or pouring a glass of wine while your wife puts up her feet those first fifteen minutes after she arrived home.

What I'm talking about is more behind the scenes. You might not be feeling well, so your wife will make a doctor's appointment for you. Or your car might need a service, so your husband takes care of it completely.

Actually, let me give you an example from my own life. Back in my younger days I used to travel a lot. As in at least one local flight per week, and two international trips per month. In between all of that I had to keep track of what piece of writing needed to be submitted to who and when.

My wife, in her infinite wisdom, set up a calendar. Not just for me, but for the whole family. Where we needed to be and when. I never asked her to do it, but she did it anyway. It made my life so much easier, and now as I write this, I can't remember if I ever thanked her for doing it. See how easy it is to take something for granted?

If you want to know if you take your partner for granted, the article suggests imagining your life without your partner (Whitbourne, 2014). Don't just imagine all the things you'll have to do yourself, but imagine your emotional wellbeing without them around. What would your future look like? I'm guessing the answer is not good.

This introspection isn't just good for you, but for your partner as well. Once you've completed this exercise, chances are you'll be more affectionate and caring with them. Perhaps they'll be motivated to do the same, which will lead to a renewed realization of why you decided to commit to each other in the first place.

Being Clingy

This is the complete opposite of the above. While some of us take our partners for granted, others need constant affirmation that everything is okay. There may not even be any signs of trouble in the relationship, but some people will still suffer from relationship anxiety.

The constant affirmation can be exhausting to the other party, eventually driving them away. While this tends to happen more in new relationships, it does happen in long-term relationships as well.

In newer relationships, it's important not to read too much into something small, and in a long-term relationship, you have years of memories to look back at to help you reach a calmer state. Don't go thinking the relationship is over simply because she forgot to give you a kiss before she left for work one morning.

Not Keeping Secrets

Basically, you should never ever talk about the body you buried in the back garden.

Only kidding, but that's the basic premise of keeping each other's secrets. As a couple, you're bound to have some secrets you share or some information that is completely private and not for anyone else's ears.

To demonstrate, I'll use examples. Let's say one of you was bullied at school, which led to years of self-esteem issues. Even to this day, your partner goes to therapy once a month, just to touch base and talk with an objective outsider.

No matter how juicy or interesting this might be to you, and no matter how long you've known your best friend, this is not the kind of information you share. It's private, and a clear step outside the boundaries of your relationship. Over time we tend to let these boundaries slip a little, giving other people a glimpse into your life. It may seem harmless, and your partner may never find out, but imagine they did. You'll have overstepped in a big way, and some trust will be lost.

The relationships you share as a couple are, if anything, even more sacred. Your finances, sex life, problems, and the like are nobody else's business but your own. And even if you do share some of these details, you should make it very clear that the information is not to be shared with anyone else.

This is particularly important in the age of social media, where people have an incessant need to share, and overshare. We made that mistake once, after sharing the news that my wife was expecting our first. Naturally, we wanted to tell our parents first, but we forgot to tell them that the news was not to be shared outside that room. In our minds, the secrecy was implied. Unfortunately, my mom had other ideas. She posted the news on Facebook and within minutes people started phoning to congratulate us. This robbed us of the joy of telling our other close relatives and friends in person.

The basic lesson here is that you should have clear boundaries, and to confirm them every once in a while. Even if your partner told you something in confidence ten years ago, it should remain a secret unless he/she decides to share it with the world.

Complaining to other people

Everybody likes to complain. Couple that with the fact that nobody's perfect either, and at some point you'll have something to complain about when it comes to your partner. They're not romantic enough, or you hate their parents, or you're just generally unhappy about how your relationship is going.

It takes some guts to tackle these topics head-on with your partner, so what do we do instead? We complain to other people. This kind of behavior may seem harmless as if you're just sharing the trials and tribulations of your relationship with your best friend, but if we dig a bit deeper we can see that it does much more damage than that.

For one, having a willing ear to listen to your relationship problems means that you'll be willing to talk. At the end of the day, that's all you'll ever talk about, making you even more negative about the state of your relationship. When all you do is complain, you forget about your partner's positive attributes, or, in other words, the reasons you stay. This constant negative imparting of information will lead to resentment quite easily.

It can also do some serious damage to your partner, because what if they ever found out that you talk about your problems behind their back? An unintended word might slip out during a conversation, or the person you talked to tells whatever to someone else. Somehow, the information manages to make it back to your spouse.

There's another evil at play here as well, and it's one I despise with a passion. Don't ever air your dirty laundry on social media. Some people come right out and explain their dissatisfaction with their partner, while others will post subtle remarks with very obvious subtones. That kind of information is not for public consumption. Not only are you breaking serious boundaries, but you lose your partner's trust immediately.

The best option when something is bothering you is to talk about it openly. And if you can't breach the subject in person, at least do it via a text to get the ball rolling. There's no need to notify your partner of your dissatisfaction with the relationship by posting your feelings on an open forum.

Passive-Aggressive Behavior

Here's another favorite of those who are too afraid to approach their relationship problems in a healthy, open way. The problem with passive-aggressive behavior is that it's not easy to identify as such. By nature, it's a dishonest way of expressing how you really feel about a topic.

It's worth stating that it can be non-hostile toward you. Let's say your partner doesn't want to go to a party, but she can't give you a clear reason why she doesn't want to go. You eventually persuade her to come anyway, but from her non-verbal signals, it's quite clear that she really doesn't want to be there. She's openly hostile to your friends, makes a point of segregating herself from the group, or constantly asks whether it's time to go home again. That's one version of passive-aggressive behavior.

This example is quite easy to recognize, which means you can actually ask her why she behaved that way. Perhaps she'll say that she's not fond of that one friend of yours who makes inappropriate jokes. One can see why she behaved that way, but there are better ways of communicating than acting rudely at a party.

Then there's the hostile kind of passive-aggressive comment, meant to hurt. Let's use mowing the lawn as an example again. You were supposed to do it, but it slipped your mind. You deserved to be called out for it, but as we discussed earlier in the book, there are nicer ways of doing it.

A hostile passive-aggressive comment will look something like this: You just spend the afternoon playing with the kids on the lawn. As soon as you come back in the house, your partner will say something along the lines of "that looked like so much fun, but just imagine how much fun it would have been if the grass was shorter." That's a comment that's meant to cut deep because you're obviously just coming off a high.

It's not that you're not guilty, but a hostile comment like that isn't the best way to approach the topic. Chances are, an entire evening is now spoiled because your happy emotional state was cut down to the knees almost immediately. It's hard not to respond to a comment like that reasonably, which inevitably leads to a fight.

A great deal of passive-aggressive behavior stems from a person's expectation that their partner should be able to read their minds, instead of them simply coming out and saying what they want. As discussed earlier in this book, you can't read your partner's mind. If you know them well enough you can tell what they are thinking when it comes to certain things, but it's impossible to always know what the other party is thinking.

My dislike for passive-aggressive behavior boils down to the amount of time it wastes. The person doing it will wait hours, and even days to act out against something they didn't like. During that time, they're not in a good place, and you're blissfully unaware that you did something wrong.

Rather just come out and say it when something's bothering you. It might lead to an argument, but at least after the argument is done the conflict is resolved.

Questioning Why You're Together

Unfortunately, this is one of the signs that a relationship might have run its course, but it depends on where it comes from.

As discussed earlier in the book, some people need constant affirmation. Their low self-esteem drives them to believe that their relationship is constantly on the rocks. This can be fixed with proper communication in a relationship, and perhaps some outside help from a therapist.

What I'm referring to here is someone who doesn't suffer from low self-esteem, but still questions the relationship. They wonder why they keep soldiering on, and whether it will still be ongoing a week, month, or year from now.

Obviously, a person like this isn't happy. You might even be that person, wondering whether you're really getting something out of this, or if you're only wasting time while the perfect person for you is still out there.

It could be one of two things. You're either taking your partner for granted, in which case you should follow the advice mentioned earlier in this chapter. Imagine your life without them and all the things you miss.

If it's not that, approach your partner with these feelings to try and find a solution. Try to discover the root of the problem, and what might be done to fix it.

It's also worth noting that questioning a relationship constantly is a clear sign that it has indeed run its course.

Low Ranking for Your Partner

Like before, when I asked you to sit and think about what your life would be like without your partner, I'd now like to ask you to sit and think about your partner's ranking within your life. In other words, in terms of importance, where do they rank?

I've made my opinion on this very clear. To me, my wife ranks as number one. She's the one I'll be spending a lifetime with, so I'll always put more work into my relationship with her than anyone else.

For many people, that's not the case. There are kids, parents, and friends to consider as well. If you rank your parents and friends above your partner, something is seriously wrong. There's a good case to be made for younger kids, so we'll ignore their role in this.

A good example would be spending an unhealthy amount of time with your family and friends, instead of with your partner. Would you rather meet your mother for brunch for the fourth week in a row than having brunch with your partner?

It's another one of those things that happen over time, most likely subconsciously. We tend to take our partners for granted, thinking that they'd be fine with us spending time with someone else. In reality, they might be sitting at home feeling unappreciated.

Not being up high enough on your list of relationships will lead to resentment.

Giving Up on Your Partner

This may be the most relevant item on this list, given the current global crisis. Millions of people lost their jobs, and at the time of writing, the world is still suffering due to the 2020 pandemic.

When times get tough we respond with fight or flight. Giving up and running away is easy, but this is when your partner needs you the most.

Now, I'm not going to pretend that it's easy. It's hard to be optimistic during tough times, and constantly reminding them that times will get better is nothing more than a soothing lie that will eventually lose its power. You need to acknowledge that times are hard, but that you can get through it together.

Leaving your partner when times are tough will not just cause emotional pain due to the breakup, but longer-lasting damage due to the rejection. They already lost their job, they're at their weakest and now they're losing you as well.

On the flip side, staying with your partner during the tough times will not only improve your relationship, but it will boost confidence levels as well. It's the ultimate expression of staying together through thick and thin, knowing that you'll always have each other no matter what happens in life.

These tough times may even improve communication between the two of you. As I mentioned earlier in the book, my wife understood what I was going through after I lost my dad. She was the one person I could talk to because she knew what I was feeling, and she was already my go-to person for discussing serious emotional matters.

Instead of letting the tough times beat your relationship down, turn it into an opportunity to grow stronger together.

Hopelessness

When something truly terrible happens in a relationship, it's usually a long, hard road to recovery. I'm not talking about arguments about who should do the dishes, or who forgot to make dinner, but the really serious stuff. Infidelity, losing a child, going broke, and losing your home…

These things happen, and we think life will never be the same again. Unfortunately, for the three things I mentioned above, that's 100% true. Life will never be the same again, but that doesn't mean you'll never be happy again.

That's exactly nine things that end most relationships according to Dr. Whitbourne, but I can think of a few other examples that are just as common, albeit not as serious.

Ignoring Bad Behavior

This usually tends to happen during the beginning of a new relationship, but it's not strictly limited to that. Examples include getting drunk at parties, fighting, and rudeness to waiters.

We ignore this kind of behavior at the beginning because we don't want to create conflict straight off the bat, even if that means upsetting third parties. While it may be uncomfortable to call a new partner out on their bad behavior, it's worth doing it. I'll use an example to illustrate how ignoring bad behavior in the short-term can do damage in the long term.

Let's say you met someone new recently, and you want to introduce him/her to your closest friends, or even your parents. The evening is going well until the conversation turns to politics. Your new partner says something mildly racist, suggesting undertones of intolerance you weren't aware of. You let it slide because it's not worth creating a big fuss in front of everyone present.

Two things will likely happen if you don't address the problem right away. First, your friends will lose some respect for you, because they know that you're not that kind of person. Secondly, because he/she got away saying whatever it is they said, they'll assume that you agree with the statement. Already this relationship is starting based on lies, which just isn't a good idea.

In long-term relationships, bad behavior seems like a non-issue. You've known this person for a decade or more, so there really aren't any surprises left. But, as I've said before, we live in difficult times. Your partner may have lost significantly during the 2020 pandemic, leading to all sorts of bad habits, such as drinking too much, stress eating, and generally just being angry at life and rude to other people because of it.

At least in this scenario, you have the freedom to call them out on it without worrying about the relationship souring. They might handle it negatively at first, but talking it through will eventually lead to them seeing that your concern stems from caring for them.

I suspect a lot of relationships will be going through this in the coming years, and it simply can't be ignored. By ignoring it, we're essentially giving the bad behavior to go-ahead to continue.

Sacrificing Other Relationships

Another example of something that usually happens in a new relationship, but that's not unheard of in long-established partnerships.

I'm not talking about telling your friends you'd rather go out on a date than hang out with them, as that's perfectly understandable. This rather has to do with what happens after you introduce your new partner to those closest to you.

In a worst-case scenario, your partner and your loved ones don't get along at all. Perhaps it's just one person they don't get on with, for whatever reason. Unfortunately, most people tend to think you only have one option in this case - choose one or the other.

That's not the case at all. Since it's a problem between them and not you, it's rather a choice they should make. You do mean something to both of them after all, and if they really do care, they'll be willing to do what is necessary to solve the problem. I advise an open, honest discussion.

Longer-term relationships are trickier. As we know, families can't get along all the time. Once your partner has become part of your family, it's only natural that he/she will eventually clash with another family member. There's no choosing between the two in this scenario, which only leaves one option. They'll just have to talk it out like adults and get over it.

Projecting

A couple is basically two people functioning as a unit, but it's always worth remembering that the two individuals involved aren't the same person. They still have unique, distinct personalities with their own world views and opinions about things.

There aren't any studies suggesting what the most common form of projecting is, but I'm willing to bet it has to do with low self-esteem and jealousy. The person with these traits will then project these emotions on to their partner. It's basically the bully effect. A bully is normally someone with low self-esteem and abuse problems at home, which is why he/she comes to school and projects these problems onto other children.

In cases where the one partner is jealous and projecting, you'll often find that there are some serious trust issues. They'll take something as innocent as getting stuck in traffic and arriving home later than usual as a sure sign of cheating.

We'll be covering low self-esteem fully in the next chapter, so you'll find your solution to this particular problem there.

Jealousy

Jealousy is a particularly destructive emotion, even if it is warranted.

It's a suffocating emotion, from both sides. One partner is constantly jealous of the attention their partner is receiving, while the other partner feels smothered by having to constantly defend themselves.

Jealousy is usually an emotion tied to people with insecurities, fear, and low self-esteem. People who have been hurt by cheating partners before will be more inclined to feel jealous when they enter a new relationship.

The reason it's so destructive is that even in a best-case scenario, one partner is constantly worried that they're going to be replaced with someone new. At its worst, jealousy can lead to emotional, and verbal abuse. There will be a need to control the other person's life. They'll need to account for every minute of their day to ensure there was no time left over to go seek a better partner.

If trust is a fundamental cornerstone in a relationship, jealousy is the acid that eats away at it. The worst thing is, it builds resentment. Over time, that which you fear the most is exactly what will happen. Your partner will eventually move on to someone who doesn't inspect their every move.

Problem is, jealousy is hard to get over. In most cases, there will be a history of cheating involved in a jealous person's life. It could just be a former partner, or it could go all the way back to their parents divorcing because of an affair.

Jealousy only goes away when you remove low self-esteem and anxiety, which isn't easy. It's essentially a sort of belief. But don't fret. As promised, we'll be looking at improving self-esteem in the next chapter thoroughly.

Envy

You'd think the natural response to a partner doing well would be pride, but quite often it's envy.

Envy, I think, is one of the most natural human emotions there is. We're bombarded with the magnificent lives of others on social media every single day. And nobody ever shares images of themselves on an off day. They tend to share images of their best days, such as when they're on holiday, receiving a reward, or celebrating the purchase of a new car.

Envy within a relationship can actually be healthy. Perhaps you have a partner who is deeply empathetic and does a lot of charity work, and you wish you were more like them. This can be an effective driving force for positive change within yourself.

Malicious envy exists as well, and 99% of the time it's work or success related. One partner is jealous that the other has achieved more than they have. They receive a higher salary, have a bigger office, or a fancier title.

I used to suffer from this a little. My title has always been "writer," while my wife has grown through the ranks of television all the way to executive producer.

Luckily, there is a quick fix for this kind of envy. It's always good to remember that a person isn't just one thing. And while we may be a writer and an executive producer while we're at work, we're lovers when we're at home. There should be no competition between lovers, only admiration for what they have achieved. Besides, it's so much easier to just be happy for your partner than to resent them for being good at what they do.

Missed Opportunities

When we don't talk openly about our feelings and dreams, we miss opportunities. You might have a great opportunity, but it will require some sacrifice from your partner. So you choose to not even talk about it, and rather let things be.

Let's say a promotion at work came up. There's a chance to go to work abroad for three years, and you'd really like to go. It does, however, mean that your partner will have to give up their job to come along. To you, this seems like too much of a sacrifice, so you just turn it down and never say a word.

Meanwhile, your partner would have loved the opportunity to embark on a journey like this. Perhaps he/she always dreamed of living in another country for a while before setting down.

Alas, you'll never know, because you never talked about it.

Smartphones

Smartphones do so much damage to us as humans that I decided to dedicate a whole division to the topic. I hate the blasted things. If I could, I'd happily go back to the days where my mobile phone could do only one thing - phone. Alas, I need easy access to e-mail, and a smartphone is just the easiest way to do that. I don't, however, have any social media apps installed on it. Allow me to explain why by using an anecdote from my own life.

Many years ago, just as smartphone cameras were beginning to replace small, mobile cameras, I found myself in Zimbabwe in a town called Vic Falls. It's named after the famous Victoria Falls, which is named after Queen Victoria. Back in the day Zimbabwe was part of the Empire and known as Rhodesia.

The falls are absolutely magnificent. That year they were in flood, adding to the majesty. It was Mother Nature at her fiercest, and one couldn't help at being in awe at the sheer power and grandeur she conjured up that day. For obvious reasons, I wanted a photograph, as did everyone else. It was actually comical, watching a long line of international tourists trying to find a spot next to the fence to take a photograph.

Next to me, however, was one of my oldest colleagues, back from my travel writing days. He just stood there and watched. I knew him as a strange, yet a lovable human being. He was one of those people that didn't speak much, but when he spoke, people listened. He'd sit quietly at a dinner table for two hours, and then he'd pipe up and say something to me along the lines of, "Ben, you should never ride your motorcycle when you're in a hurry."

I loved him for his strange, awkward nature, and the fact that he owned it completely. He seemed to live in another world, which I think was more beautiful than ours. In any case, I asked him why he didn't take any photographs of the falls that day, beyond what he needed to publish his story later on. His answer changed my life, and the way I look at smartphones. "You know," he said, "I can see what's going to happen with these things. We're going to start viewing the world through a small screen, and why would you do that when the real actual thing (in this case the falls) is right there in front of you?" He can add fortune teller to his list of many talents because that's exactly what happened.

A few years after that, my wife and I were in Paris. The Louvre wasn't too busy that day, so we decided to finally go see La Jaconde, more famously known as the Mona Lisa. The Louvre is very much geared for people who only got there to see her. She has more signs pointing in her direction than anything else in that place. We quickly found the room, and what I saw was the strangest chaos you can imagine. People would spend 10 minutes fighting to get to the front, take a selfie with her, and move on. I didn't do that. I fought my way to the front and spent a good 15 minutes just looking at her, trying to see all of the intricate details that I've read about over the years. I don't have a single photo of Mona Lisa, or me visiting her, and I'm weirdly proud of that. It's a moment in time that was never recorded, never to be repeated.

I'm not saying that I'm not guilty of taking thousands of photographs of my own. I just checked and I have exactly 1367 photographs on my phone. It's either a photograph of my child, or a classic car I spotted on the street.

But the big takeaway from this for me is to always live in the moment. Smartphones made us forget to do that. It's almost as if we're not doing things for our own pleasure anymore, but rather doing them so we can post an image online to say that we've done something. That's my first gripe with smartphones.

The second is the fact that they've robbed us of alone time. Whenever we find ourselves alone for an hour or so, we never seem to just sit and quietly exist. You pull out the phone to see what's happening elsewhere.

This is such a pity because alone time is so good for relationships. Firstly, alone time gives you the opportunity to think by yourself without any outside interference. There's nobody there to question your thoughts, which is a good thing. It means finding your own point of view on whatever it is you're thinking about.

So far I've mentioned thinking about your relationship multiple times, and alone time is the perfect time for that. Perhaps you need to sit and think about what your life would be like without your partner, or you need to remind yourself not to be envious of them.

Instead, the smartphone comes out.

Let's break the damage the smartphone does to a relationship down into further subcategories.

Smartphone Addiction

Is smartphone addiction a real thing? Yes, it even has a scientific name. The fear of being without your phone is called nomophobia. It works the same way as any other addiction. Using your phone releases some feel-good chemicals like dopamine, and once you build up a taste for it, you want some more. And we really do want more.

Kommando Tech compiled the most shocking smartphone-related facts in an article titled, How Much Time Does the Average Person Spend on Their Phone? (Milenkovic, 2020).

Americans spend roughly 5.4 hours a day on their phones. Millennials spend around 48 minutes texting, while Baby Boomers spend 30 minutes on this activity.

As if these statistics aren't shocking enough, let's put them in perspective within an average day. You spend roughly eight hours sleeping, and eight hours at work.

That's already 16 hours of the day. Adding the phone time takes you to 21 hours, which only leaves a total of three hours to get ready in the morning, eat breakfast, lunch, and dinner, commute, and spend time with the family. To be honest, we're probably on our phones while doing most of the activities above, so it's not as drastic as that, but we can't deny the fact that our phones are robbing us of time we should be spending doing something more useful. It's oddly ironic, isn't it? A device invented to bring us closer together is helping us grow apart. There have never been so many people on the planet as there is right now, and yet we've never had so many people feel so alone.

Relationship Anxiety

Over the course of this book, we've seen many communication problems stem from low self-esteem. And smartphones coupled with access to social media only adds fuel to the fire.

Imagine what a person suffering from anxiety, especially about their relationship, must feel like while scrolling through a timeline feed of happy couples getting engaged, married, or having their first child. The immediate thought is, "why don't I have that?"

We tend to forget the number one rule when it comes to social media. People only ever share when life is at its absolute best. They never share the in-between bits, showing you that they're just as normal as you are. You might see a post of a happy couple dining out at a sushi restaurant, but what you didn't see was the 30-minute argument about where they were going to eat that night.

And the worst part is, you're probably looking at all of this stuff, wondering about how strong your own relationship is, while your partner is sitting on the couch across from you doing exactly the same thing.

Losing Contact

As I mentioned just now, those with high levels of anxiety, which is a large portion of the population these days, live in constant fear of losing their partner. Worst of all is the fact that you're worried about your relationship while staring at a phone, while your partner is in the same room.

Understand that social media is addictive. It's programmed to be that way. Your phone probably knows more about you than anyone else on the planet. I'll give you an example. Writing this book requires a lot of research into low self-esteem, communication, and basically everything else we've covered so far. The moment I open any kind of social media app on my desktop, the advertising will be targeted according to that. It knows exactly what you want, and it will keep on giving you that.

There was a time I was semi-addicted to it myself. Not so much that I'd constantly check in every few minutes, but at night I'd run through what everyone had to say that day, and comment on what interested me most. Much to the dismay of my wife, who was sitting right across from me waiting to tell me about her day. Eventually, she joined the club, rather than fighting against it. So, there we were. Two people sharing a room, not talking to each other because our phones were more interesting.

Until the day my wife told me it felt like she hasn't seen me in days, even though I didn't go anywhere. We realized what the problem was, and we implemented a system, which I'll discuss later.

I know for a fact we're not the only couple who has/had this problem. I'm fascinated to see the low levels of interaction between couples sitting in a restaurant. Rather than enjoying each other's company, and ignoring the phone, they'd pick it up the moment it buzzed or pinged. What's even sadder is that it's just considered the norm these days. It seems to be totally cool to interrupt a discussion to check your phone.

Losing Intimacy

Smartphones have invaded the sanctity of the bedroom. After we got married and had to decorate the house, my wife had one rule: We'd never have a television in our room, because to her it was one of the saddest things in life. A couple's bedroom is a sacred place. It's where they share their most intimate discussions, and it's where they have sex most of the time. There's no room for any distraction in the bedroom.

Yet the same thing happens as I mentioned above. Instead of getting intimate after the kids have gone to bed, we turn to the smartphone to tell us what's hot. A month goes by and you wonder why there's this sudden gap between you and your partner. You can't put a finger on it, but it feels like you haven't touched base in ages.

Your phone is the reason why.

Regret

We all likely know or have heard of a relationship that was broken up because one partner found an old flame on a social media platform.

The reason is a breakdown in communication and regret. Instead of talking about our problems, which is a tough activity that takes time and effort, we turn to social media for a shot of dopamine to make us feel better.

We start searching for a time when we are happy, instead of trying to find a solution to the problem that keeps us from being happy right now. In short, we're living in the past. This inevitably leads you to stumble across the profile of an ex, and you start wondering what your life would have been like if that relationship didn't end when it did. She was never this strict with me, and she never expected me to mow the lawn, or help with the baby, or the dishes, or anything else for that matter. We just had fun.

Yes, you did, but only because you were in a different phase of your life back then. It was college. You weren't living with her, there were no dishes and there was no baby. Your main priority back then was scraping enough money together to buy a beer and some cigarettes.

It's important to understand that you miss that feeling of freedom, and not the person tied to the freedom you had at that time in your life. You're projecting all that happiness you felt back then onto one person, and you start thinking about leaving your current relationship and going back to that one.

I don't believe in regret. I think it's a useless emotion. I do feel it sometimes, but I always remind myself that my life has never been better than it is at that moment. Each phase of a person's life comes with challenges. Back then it was money for beer and cigarettes, and now it's keeping an entire family happy while juggling the many responsibilities that come with adulting.

If you're inclined to do this, ask yourself one important question: What were the rewards? It's perfectly fine to feel nostalgic sometimes, thinking about a time when life was... easier. But the reward was just a beer and a pack of cigarettes. The rewards you reap from putting in the work as an adult, especially when it comes to your relationship, is so much better than anything that came before.

How to Get Rid of This Addiction

Knowing that we had a semi-serious phone addiction problem, my wife and I implemented a rather drastic strategy at home. We have a basket at the entrance of the house, and when the day is finished and everyone is home safe, the phones go in the basket.

But what about emergencies, I hear you ask. We have a burner phone for that. Just a basic thing that can make calls and everyone near and dear to us have that number. It's to be used in case of emergencies, and it's kept on my nightstand. For us, the fix was as simple as that.

Success offers a more comprehensive guide in an article called *12 Steps to Breaking Smartphone Addiction* (Pietrzak, 2019).

Most of the advice is relatively straight-forward and easy to implement. You can remove some of the more time-consuming apps, turn off notifications, and leave it elsewhere when you have dinner with the family or a conversation with your spouse.

The more serious steps include admitting you have a problem, and realizing that the phone is not your boss. You have total and complete control over it, so exercise that control and switch it off for a bit. Take a break from it. Just a small break at first, and then eventually a longer break.

It also mentions paying attention to all the other wonderful things around you and making a list of all the non-phone-related things you like doing. Instead of wasting a Sunday afternoon on social media, why not have a picnic in the garden with the wife and kids. They'll surely enjoy the attention, and you'll get more out of it than doing a quiz to find out what kind of fruit you are.

The main switch you have to make is to only pick up that phone with intent, in other words, you have a task to complete and you need the phone to do it. Like sending a work mail, or phoning your mom. Ask yourself that question every time you pick your phone up. Do I actually have a specific task in mind, or am I reaching for it subconsciously, or to waste time on meaningless apps?

Chapter 6:

Be a Better Communicator

In this chapter we'll be moving away from relationships here and there, but keep in mind that it's all applicable at the end of the day. The goal is to make you an effective communicator to achieve success not just in your relationship, but in other areas as well.

By now I've identified a lot of problems a relationship can have, and as you've no doubt noticed, many of them have the same solution - more effective communication. So that's what we'll focus on achieving in this chapter.

The Walden University in Minnesota offers an easy seven-step guide in its article, How to Be an Effective Communicator in 7 Easy Steps (Anonymous, 2020). It mentions at the start that effective communication breeds both confidence and optimism, which could easily fix 90% of the problems mentioned in the previous chapter.

Here's how you become an effective communicator in seven steps. We'll be delving deeper than this, later on, getting even more specific.

Have a Clear Objective

You need to know what you want to achieve in order to choose the right way to communicate. Having a clear objective will also keep your message on track, and stop you from branching off onto something else when you get nervous. While on the topic of being nervous, having a clear objective means you can prepare. With preparation comes confidence, and confidence is key.

Listen Properly

I discussed this properly earlier on, so we won't dive too deep into it again. Always remember to not only focus on what you want to communicate but what the other party wants to communicate back to you. As I said, one of the biggest mistakes we make is already formulating a response while the other person is talking, when you should actually be listening to what they're saying. Communicating is so much more effective when every party is actively involved, whether speaking or listening.

Watch Your Own Body Language

What your body is saying is just as important as what your mouth is communicating.

Imagine a one-on-one conversation with someone. In one scenario they're slumped back in the chair, head to the side, and with their hands folded in front of them. It's quite a hostile posture, and it already sets the tone of the conversation. Now imagine that same conversation where the person is seated straight up, or standing casually. It's a posture that says they're here, willing to listen and engage.

Different Tactics for Different Audiences

Think about all the people in your life, and how the way you communicate with them already differs. You don't talk to your husband/wife the same way you talk to a child. It would come across as condescending.

You already instinctively know that there are certain things you can't do or say in front of certain people, but now it's time to take that a step further.

When you have something important to say to somebody, consider their personality traits, and how you can adapt your message for them. Not only is it a sign of respect, but the message will be better understood.

Pacing

How many times have you been involved in an argument where you struggle to get a word in? I'm sure all of us have at some point. So, when you do get your turn to speak, you throw out all your counter-arguments in rapid succession, hoping that a few of them will stick. This isn't effective at all.

You need to slow the conversation down, otherwise, some things will get lost in translation. If the other person insists on keeping up the rapid-fire, stand your ground. Keep the pace slow, and repeat the point you're trying to make. At some point, they'll have no choice but to match your speed if the conversation is going to go anywhere.

Timing

It's amazing what you can achieve by timing things right.

Let's say you need a new couch for the living room because the old one is getting a bit saggy, and smelly because of the dog lying on it all day long. Bombarding your spouse with this request just as they get home is not the best tactic. They've just spent eight hours at work, and likely an hour in traffic to get home. They likely just want to fall on that couch and enjoy what little comfort it still has left in it. Rather wait a few hours until the house is quiet, and breach the subject over a glass of wine. "Now wouldn't this be more fun on a brand-new couch? These old ones really are starting to be a pain in the back."

Similarly, you should know when to talk about something serious. Perhaps the time has come to discuss having another child. The last thing you want to do is ambush your partner when they don't have the time to sit down for what will likely be a long discussion. I mean, dropping a bomb like that 15 minutes before your wife/husband has to leave for work is not ideal.

Clarity

We tend to think that we need to substantiate the way we feel about something before we can actually start talking about it. This is true for both old and new relationships, and I'll give examples for both.

First, the short term relationship that one partner wants to firmly establish as exclusive. You say that you've been dating for so long and that you've really enjoyed your time together. You can really see this going somewhere, but you don't want to put any pressure on the other person. "We don't have to label it or anything, I just think we should perhaps stop seeing other people."

This roundabout way of arguing leaves room for misinterpretation. Using the word "perhaps" means there may still be wiggle room left for seeing other people.

Be clear in what you want, and don't be ashamed of it. Most people will appreciate the honesty, as they're most likely wondering about the same thing. And if you don't agree that your relationship is there yet, at least that bit of knowledge is now out in the open.

In long-term relationships, it is easier to just be brutally honest with your partner, but there are certain sensitive topics that are tough to breach. I'll give you an example from my own life. My wife's sister lives in another country, and twice a year they'll come to visit. My wife knows me well enough to know that I'm an extremely quiet person and that I don't like having people, with the exception of my own family, in my space for too long.

For the first few times, they needed a place to stay, my wife would always start the conversation by saying, "you know, Jana is coming to town." She usually followed this by saying, "you know, hotels are so expensive these days." I'd just roll my eyes, and tell her to just ask me what she wanted to ask me.

For the record, I have no problem having my sister in law and her husband here for a month. I count them as family and they're a joy to have around. But this example perfectly points out how two people with degrees in communication still make the mistake of asking for something quite simple by using an elaborate story.

More Tips for Effective Couple's Communication

Everything you read above is aimed at making you a more effective communicator overall. If you read between the lines carefully, you'll see that every single one of them is applicable to life in general. You can even use the tips above to ask your boss for a raise. Choose the right method for communicating, choose the right time to do so, and then be clear about why you think you deserve it. You'd be amazed at what you can achieve with the seven steps above.

But now I'd like to move back into the sphere of relationships, with more targeted, small things you can do to improve communication in your relationship.

Touch

Seems like a small thing, but it can pack a powerful punch. If you've been with someone for a while, you probably have a routine for when one of you arrives at home. You shout a greeting from the door, excusing yourself because you desperately need to use the bathroom after your commute.

I'd like to challenge you to do more. When you arrive home, embrace your significant other and kiss them like you're kissing them for the first time. "But there might be kids in the room," I hear you say. So what? It's just a kiss, and it sets a good example for them as well. Few things make a child feel safer than knowing their parents are still very much in love. And talking as a man with a son specifically, I always try and set an example, hoping that he'll show his wife the same level of affection and attention one day.

In addition to all of the above, touching is one of those actions that release those feel-good hormones. Just what one needs after a long day of work, as it's nature's own stress-relief medicine.

Don't Interrogate

The way you phrase questions can often come across as hostile, which will inevitably make your partner defensive, possibly leading to an argument.

Once again, mowing the lawn pops up as an example. Instead of asking "why the hell didn't you mow the lawn?," rather go for, "I was just wondering why you didn't mow the lawn." It conveys the same message, just with less hostility.

Don't be Smart With Your Partner

It's not often you come across partners who have the same job. They may be in the same industry, but it's almost never the exact same job.

Now, every job comes with its own insider lingo. I'll use my relationship as an example here. My wife and I both work in the media, but while I do the adventure writing, she does television production. Both jobs come with their own insider lingo. I'll often have to explain why my adventure ground to a halt due to a car malfunctioning. And while I can describe the process of internal combustion in minute detail, my wife has no clue how it works, neither does she want to know. So instead of telling her that a sensor in the catalytic converter was acting up, and because of that the car went into limp mode, I'd rather just tell her the car broke.

Similarly, I know they work on different color scripts, according to how many rewrites there are. So instead of her telling me they're on level pink, she just tells me that she's going to be a bit late because she needs to do some rescheduling.

I get that it's normal to want to sound smart in a conversation. It feels particularly good when you meet new people, and you want them to think that your job is insanely important. But there's no need to pretend in front of your partner. They know what you do for a living, and are most likely proud of you.

So the next time your wife asks you how your day went, don't say, "well, cylinder number five isn't firing in the correct order, so I have to take the whole block apart." Just tell her that you're having car problems and that you'll sort it out in no time.

Understand Your Partner's Love Language

Most of you have likely heard of love languages. It's basically the five ways in which a person expresses and feels loved. The five types are gifts, words of affirmation acts of service, touch, and quality time. These categories are self-explanatory, so I won't get into them.

It's easy to reject it as mumbo jumbo, but I do think there is something to it. I wouldn't base a whole relationship just on a person's love language, but it is nice to know what they appreciate.

There's no doubt that I'm a gift-giver. I hate spending money on myself, but I have no problem swiping my card when I see something I know one of my close family members will love. Oddly, I'm not bothered too much about receiving gifts, but being an anxious person, I do appreciate words of affirmation. Luckily, my wife is extremely good at that.

It's an interesting theory you can Google, but as I said, I wouldn't base my entire relationship and the way I communicate based on love language alone.

Be Enthusiastic With Them

I know this can be hard, especially when you don't really care about your partner's hobby. Obviously, you'll be enthusiastic when something life-changing happens, like a promotion, pregnancy, or a new house, but I'm not talking about those things.

The reason I know this is hard is that I don't understand my wife's hobby, and she doesn't get mine either. She has a thing for stationery. She can spend hours in a stationary store and will come home almost bouncing with elation because she found a collection of pencils at an extremely reasonable price.

I'm a bit of a fanatic when it comes to classic cars. In fact, I think I may have a problem. I'll spot an old classic car for super cheap, buy it, and then spend around a year fixing it only to sell it for more or less what I bought it for. It doesn't make sense, but I love it. My wife couldn't care less. As long as my latest project and tools aren't in her way, I'm good.

At least we both have the decency to acknowledge that our hobbies don't make sense to each other, but that doesn't mean we have to fake elation when the other person finds something that makes them happy.

You see, it's not about cheap pencils or cars, but rather what they represent. They represent happiness, and how can you not match their level of enthusiasm when they find something that gives them joy.

Leave Small Talk for Strangers

The standard greeting for somebody you know in passing always goes something along the lines of, "hi, how are you." They'll say "good, how are you?", and then you'll respond "good" back. Then the conversation is over.

That should never happen with your partner. You should always make a concentrated effort to converse on a deeper level because if the greeting above resembles your greeting after a day without each other, something is seriously wrong.

Don't ask superficial questions. Rather ask them to tell them about their day. Did anything interesting happen? Did Bob from accounts fall off his chair again?

Small talk is called small talk for a reason. It's basically just good manners to acknowledge someone you know in passing. The whole conversation is designed to be over as quickly as possible, and that's not something you want in your relationship.

Only having superficial conversations with your partner is one of those things that will eventually lead you down the path of growing apart. Before you know it, you're completely out of touch with him/her, and pretty soon you find yourself living with a stranger.

Talk Them Up

Yet another small thing you can implement to make your partner feel appreciated.

Whenever you introduce them to somebody new, say something about them that you appreciate. "Meet my husband, Ben. He's got this insanely cool talent for remembering useless, yet interesting information, so you definitely want to spend some time talking to him."

The same is true when it comes to old friends and family. If your partner is too humble or shy to talk about their achievements, do it for them. As we saw earlier in this book, self-esteem and recognition are one of the most basic human desires, and by doing this one small thing, you can boost your partner's confidence so much. And they'll love you even more for doing it.

Create a Safe Space

I'm not talking about a safe space one of you can go to when life gets too tough. This is rather about creating a space where both of you know some sharing is about to be done.

We have a nice setup, just outside our bedroom. It's a little garden, completely blocked off from the rest of the property. In it are some potted plants, and a bench.

It's our own little haven, far away from the neighbors, and anyone else living in our house at any given time.

While this space is often used just to sit and relax, when either of us says "we have to talk," the talking is done out there. It generally just sets the mood. While the discussion will likely be serious in nature, it will be had in a safe place that you created together. It already adds a bit of calmness to the mix, which means you'll be less inclined to go off on a tangent and say things you shouldn't say.

Find Common Ground

It may not seem like it, but you can find common ground in every argument. This is especially true when it comes to long-term relationships.

Arguments, by definition, stem from opposing views. Let's say, for example, a couple is in disagreement over what school they should send their child to. The mother wants to send their child to a private school, while the father wants the child to attend his alma mater, which happens to be a public school.

The mother argues that she wants the best education they can possibly afford, while the father knows from experience what kind of education his child will receive. Perhaps he's even worried about the stigma that comes with a private school and doesn't want his child to be stereotyped from a young age.

While they are coming at this from opposing sides, there is a common ground. Both of them want what's best for the child. That's already a good place to start. From there you can hash it out further, but if you can find one or two things you already agree on, the rest of the argument should be civil and reasonable enough.

Sex and Intimacy

I find it extremely strange that we struggle to communicate on a deeper level with the person that arguably knows us better than anyone else. We should be able to tell them anything, without fear of being shunned. You are compatible in almost every other way, so why would you be scorned when it comes to intimacy and sex. We'll delve into that a bit later, but for now, I just want to talk about sex and new relationships, mostly because there are health implications and a whole new set of rules.

Sex in a New Relationship

There are various reasons why you should have an open discussion about sex in a new relationship. The most obvious reason is consent. For far too long now has consent been a grey area, but recent movements like #metoo and #menaretrash have put the spotlight on the issue.

Before you do anything, make sure you have consent. This is non-negotiable. Luckily, younger people are more open to talking about sex, and sexual health.

On the topic of health, it may seem awkward to ask someone to get tested for sexually transmitted diseases, but it is in both your best interests. The same is true when it comes to birth control. It may seem awkward to discuss what methods of birth control you'll be using, but, trust me on this, an unwanted pregnancy is way more awkward.

The best way to get over this is to go to the doctor together to get tested, and or talk about birth control options. That way you're both starting with a blank page, showing that previous sexual engagements don't matter and that your only focus is on being healthy in this current relationship.

Talking Intimacy and Sex Long-Term

The first thing you need to remember is that sex and intimacy are not the same things. These are often confused because sex is an intimate act, but intimacy stretches so far beyond just the purely physical act of love.

Intimacy is being tender, open, affectionate, and vulnerable. Allow me to better explain the difference between sex and intimacy by creating an imaginary situation.

A couple just had amazing sex. He arrived home to find his wife in the mood after a few drinks. Tough day at the office, you know. They immediately fall into it, and 15 minutes later they decide to go for a walk in the park to cool off. While in the park, they quietly walk. For a brief second, they turn to each other, smile, and squeeze each other's hands. That's intimacy. An emotional yet invisible link between two people who share a very deep connection.

Over the course of a few years, intimacy is easily lost. The above scenario is interrupted by longer working hours after a promotion, the arrival of children, and just more adulting responsibilities in general. And once intimacy has been lost, it can be tricky to get back again. I think mostly because people are too ashamed to admit that they've lost it.

Here's how you get it back.

The first step is to start asking different questions. Instead of following the normal routine of asking how the day at the office was, throw them a curveball and ask something like, "what don't I know about you?" It's a question that will likely intrigue them, especially if you use the right tone of voice. It will be fairly obvious that you want to start a conversation that's much deeper than a one that requires yes or no answers. Then you can simply take it from there.

You might think that you know absolutely everything there is to know about your partner, but I promise you, you don't. My wife only recently found out that I had a deep-rooted fear of snakes after one bit me when I was a child. In the 14 years we've known each other, the topic just never came up. And then we see a snake in the wild, and I go absolutely crazy. There she was, laughing at me for standing on the roof of the car, refusing to get off because of a rolled-up snake the size of an Oreo.

And don't forget that we change as we get older, and we find new things that interest us. I'm currently fascinated with my family lineage, and I'm not even sure that my wife knows about it yet. It could even be something simpler than that. Outside your office, you might have discovered the best food truck in America, but it hasn't come up yet because you never bothered to tell, and your wife never bothered to ask.

Don't be afraid to go out there with these questions. Ask your partner about their fears, hopes, dreams, and what they still find attractive about you. I'm willing to bet that the answers will surprise you. Best of all, it will kick off what will hopefully be a discussion lasting weeks, taking you back to a time where you were intimately connected on an emotional level.

The second tip has come up before. You need to create a safe space, far removed from the scenes that play out in front of you on a daily basis. This space will put you at ease, and as you talk it will eventually create an expectation that only intimate thoughts and moments are to be shared there. Don't forget to touch while you're talking. Not touching each other in an intimate place, but rather just holding hands.

The hardest part is going to be to take that first step to improve intimacy. At that moment you might feel so daft, but remember that vulnerability plays a big role in intimacy. Your partner might not respond as you were hoping, but keep on committing to it. The results will be worth so much more than that few minutes you feel daft.

If this doesn't work, you can always seek professional help. Intimacy plays such a big role in the way we communicate with each other. It's during intimate moments we get to see a person for who they really are, and without that, you essentially just have the basic outline of your partner. That's no way to go through life.

Talking about sex is even tougher, which I find so difficult to understand. The act itself is so intimate, and you've done it a thousand times. There's literally no part of your partner's body that you haven't seen. And for some reason, we struggle to bring it up in conversation. Perhaps it's because it happens less and less. Everyone goes through a dry spell once in a while, and we don't know how to get back in action because we don't know how to communicate our feelings on the topic properly.

First, I want to start with two things you should never, ever do. The first being simply trying something new in the bedroom without your partner's consent or even a warning. While it may look good on the television screen, your wife might not respond positively to receiving a smack on the bottom. Basically, don't use *50 Shades of Grey* as a self-help guide.

The second thing you should never do is talk about sex at an inappropriate time. Nobody wants to talk about sex when they're obviously not in the mood, nor do they want to have that discussion the moment they walk in the door and say hello. But the absolute worst time to do it is right after you've had sex.

You might be wondering why. It seems like such a perfect time to talk about it, considering that you've just done the most intimate thing one can do with another person. Take a second to think about how it might come across to your partner. You just had sex, and now the other person wants to talk about how you could possibly improve your sex life. If I were that other person, I'd take that conversation as a negative review of my performance.

When you eventually have the talk, ensure you do two things. Talk about how you feel, so it doesn't come across as you blaming them for having a lackluster sex life. You also need to evaluate your own performance. I'm speaking to the men here, specifically. I know we're visual creatures and it doesn't take a lot to get us excited, but women don't experience sex the same way. You need to remember to dish out the compliments, touch her even when you're not after sex, give her the occasional surprise embrace, or just simply tell her that you love her.

Remember that you have history, so focus on that. Your sex life may be in a slump at the moment, but it wasn't always like that. Think back to when you just met and you couldn't keep your hands off of each other. What did you do then that you don't do now? Use descriptive language, and eventually, the awkwardness will fall away.

As for the overall awkwardness of talking about sex, there is an easy way to approach the topic without being quite as forward. Sex is all around us these days. We see it on billboards, television, and even social media.

A sex scene in a television show or movie could be a great conversation starter. You could ask your partner if whatever is happening on screen is something they might be interested in. It might not be, but at least you started a conversation about it...

Most of the time all you need is just one small change. More adventurous couples can go a bit further and investigate sex toys, and books with crazy sexual positions, but for most of us, a few small changes will work wonders. Routine is the main killer of passion, and by simply making one small change you've already shattered that routine.

Finally, now that you've broken through that ceiling, keep on talking about it. Don't let it slip away and get awkward again.

Low Self-Esteem

During the course of this book, two things popped up on a regular basis - not listening, and low self-esteem. I'd go as far as saying that 90% of all communication problems in relationships can be blamed on low self-esteem.

Unfortunately, low self-esteem isn't something you can easily fix within five minutes. Low self-worth is something that takes years to develop. It can date as far back as being bullied at school, all the way through to the few serious relationships you've had before you met the one. Because it's such a serious topic, I'll be approaching it from two sides. First I'd like you to look at all the methods you can use to boost your own self-esteem, and then we'll move on to the methods you can use to do the same for your partner.

Psychology Today has two fantastic articles on these topics, with the first being *8 Steps to Improving Your Self-Esteem* (Abrams, 2017).

How to Boost Your Own Self-Esteem

The first step is to accept that you have a problem with low self-esteem. By accepting that you have this problem, you immediately take away some power from those negative thoughts that keep on popping up in your head. Always remind yourself that they're nothing more than thoughts as well. Thoughts mean nothing, it's facts that matter. You thinking you're not funny enough is just a thought, not a verified fact. Don't give thoughts more power than they deserve.

You also have the power to change your story or at least the version of the story you tell yourself in your mind. You know your history best, and you also have nothing to hide from yourself. Look back at everything that led you to believe that you weren't good enough, and ask yourself if you truly and honestly believe it.

Perhaps you've just heard the same untrue negative comment so many times that you started believing it yourself. According to the article, it's a good idea to spend one-minute writing positive things about yourself (Abrams, 2017). This kind of positive reinforcement can be a powerful tool against those thoughts that constantly bring you down.

We've touched on this next piece of advice before, but it's worth repeating. Don't compare yourself to what you see on social media. People never share the in-between struggles of life, like trying to have five minutes alone in the bathroom without a toddler trying to interrupt. But they do share a beautifully edited photo of their whole family on the way to church. Think about this realistically. You have a toddler, so you know what it takes to get them ready for that one single snapshot that makes your life seem so perfect. Social media isn't a true reflection of the real world. Get the idea that it is out of your head.

Unfortunately, not all comparisons to other people happen online. I have this annoying neighbor who runs marathons, does cycle races, and who just seems unbelievably good at all sports. I struggle with him every single day because my office just happens to look out on his front lawn. First, he does his stretches, and then he goes and runs for an hour. He waves at me every morning as he comes back, and I wave back just as friendly. Deep within I'm boiling, because if I had to run, I'd barely reach the end of my driveway before I fell down dead. Some of us just aren't athletic, but we do have other talents.

When you start comparing yourself to other people, you tend to focus on the stuff you're not good at. What you should be doing is propping yourself up, and reminding yourself of your other talents. I might not be able to run for an hour, but I can write a book. If I ever found out my neighbor could do that as well, I don't know what I'd do.

While we're on the topic of running, exercise is a good way to boost self-confidence. Not because it makes you healthier, though that is a nice side-effect. It's actually a mental thing. Taking care of your physical health empowers you. I do have some good news for all you other non-runners out there. You can basically do anything, so long as you do it alone and for self-care reasons. And yes, sufficient sleep also counts.

Get rid of any bitterness you may have in your life. This could be an ex-partner or a family member that did something to upset you. By clinging on to those negative feelings, you get stuck in an infinite loop. Some days you'll be angry at them, other days you'll wonder whether you're to blame. In any case, holding on to those feelings is holding you back. Let it go, and start a new life based on positive vibes.

Finally, remember that you are not your possessions, or your job, or your car. You are not defined by these things. You are defined by what you put out into the world, which is why you need to forget about comparing yourself to others, holding on to any bitterness, and constantly trying to remind yourself of why you're a failure. Start fresh and realize that you have the potential to put some positivity out into the world. Once you start doing that, those self-esteem levels will start to rise.

How to Boost Your Partner's Self-Confidence

If you notice that a lot of the disagreements in your relationship are based on your partner's low self-esteem, there are a few things you can do. The main idea is to get them to see themselves as you see them.

Psychologist Alice Boyes wrote an article for Psychology Today titled, *7 Ways to Give Your Partner a Boost* (Boyes, 2015).

The first tip is so simple that I think it should just form part of the daily routine within any relationship. What you need to do is compliment a body part, but, and this is important guys, not the body parts you're thinking of. You need to be aware of what your partner feels self-conscious about. Perhaps they have an issue with their hair, or they don't like the way their ears are formed. As we get older, we also tend to develop body issues we never had before. I have a belly that I didn't have when I was 27.

Take notice of what it is that's bothering your partner, and compliment that specific body part. Just don't make it seem that obvious, or it could come across as disingenuous.

You could also try and compliment a body part that they've never thought of as attractive before. I don't know what your wife/husband looks like, so I can't help you with any specifics, but I can give you an example from my relationship. My wife has a cute dimple on her lower back, just above her bottom. Every once in a while I like to remind her of how much I love it.

Another way to help them is to take note of the kind of clothes and colors that make them look good. I'll give you another example from my life. My wife has green eyes, so anything on the blue or green color spectrum makes her eyes pop.

Let them know that they look good in that color, or style of clothes. You can also take it a step further and make things intimate. Buy your spouse some lingerie, and then compliment her body. Like I said, as we grow older we become more aware that we don't have the sexy, sleek bodies we once had. Knowing that your partner still has the hots for you after all these years offers a healthy dose of self-confidence.

On a psychological level, think of something that your partner introduced to your life that made it so much better. You can just thank them for finding that decent taco joint you regularly visit, but I don't think that has enough weight to it.

Perhaps they motivated you to try yoga or convinced you to stop smoking. In my case, my wife introduced me to religion. As I mentioned, I came from an agnostic family, so I had no frame of reference. I'm still not sure about the whole religion thing, but I do enjoy the sense of community that comes with going to church. I also think receiving an inspiring speech once a week is a fairly good idea. It doesn't really matter what it is, as long as it made a notable difference in your life. Thank them for it, and watch how it boosts their self-confidence. There's no better feeling than knowing you helped another person achieve something significant in their life.

Coupled with that, you can think of something they do that makes you feel good about yourself. My wife often gives me a pinch on the bum when I'm doing the dishes. It's her way of saying thanks in a non-verbal way, and it makes me feel good. I'm sure you have a similar way of showing affection that's unique to your own relationship. Let your partner know that you appreciate it, and how good it makes you feel.

Compliment not only their taste in things but also in friends. Tell them you really enjoyed that new album they recommended. And when you spend time with their friends, tell them that they made some really good selections. The connection here is obvious. Good people tend to find each other, so by association, your partner feels good about themself as well.

Finally, compliment their sense of humor, even if it is a bit dark. One of the main characteristics we look for in partners is a good sense of humor. It's psychology 101. We like being around the people that make us laugh because it releases those feel-good hormones. Let them know that they do that for you, and they'll get an instant boost.

Communication Exercises to Try at Home

What would this book be without a few activities you can try in the comfort and safety of your own home. All of them are designed to encourage communication and improve intimacy.

Use an Egg Timer

Not only is this a great way to get 10 minutes worth of uninterrupted talking time, but it's also a great time to practice active listening. Set the timer to 10 minutes, and just start talking. The listener may only respond via non-verbal methods, which is also a great exercise. Between turns, you can have open and honest discussions, empathize with each other, and reflect and apologize.

Keep a Shared Diary

Not for long, reflective pieces on life in general, but rather a book where you each write down something flattering about the other person on a daily basis. Just imagine how invigorating it could be to start a day this way.

Give Treats

I touched on the love languages earlier, and here's a neat way to incorporate them into your life. Take turns receiving a treat from your partner, if not once a day, at least once a week. As a reminder, the love languages are gifts, quality time, physical touch, words of affirmation, and actions of service.

Examples of these treats include a ten-minute hug, the occasional unexpected gift, a 30-minute shower or bath together, or even a 30-minute bath alone while you do something useful around the house.

Sit in Silence

This is an excellent non-verbal exercise. You sit in complete silence for a few minutes, making eye contact the whole time. You're only allowed to communicate via non-verbal means. When the time is up, you can discuss what you thought about. I bet some interesting conversations will start as a result of this.

Share a Story

You might think that you know everything about each other, but I guarantee you don't. Both my wife and I have degrees in communication, and she only found out about my snake phobia after nearly 15 years of being together.

Whether it's a story of joy or a story of sorrow, it doesn't matter. The idea is to actively listen to your partner and learn more about their non-verbal cues, tone, and the way they express excitement or sadness when talking. This knowledge, as you know by now, will be infinitely helpful in any relationship.

Make Lists

This is a great activity if you're in need of some love, or if you sense your partner might be in need of some affection. Take a piece of A4 paper, head in a different direction, and make a list of all the things you love about each other.

Or, if you have a sense of humor about your relationship, and you think you can handle it, make a list of the things that annoy you. Nothing serious, mind you, but rather playful things, like the way your partner always has to smell something before they eat it.

Share Your Playlist

Music has this magical way of evoking an emotional response. At some point in your life, you must have been driving while listening to something sad and couldn't help but tear up a bit.

Love songs are a great way of expressing emotions you struggle to put into words. You might find a new song that you think perfectly captures how you feel about your partner, and playing it to them is nearly as good as telling them how you feel.

This activity can last for hours and usually ends up sparking a bout of nostalgia as you listen to the songs that were popular when you were dating or the song you first danced to at your wedding.

Best enjoyed with a bottle of wine.

High-Low

A nice, easy way to touch base with your partner on a daily basis. This can be done easily as you lie in bed, or when having a bath together. This basic exercise just requires you and your partner to share the lowest point of your day, as well as the highlight of your day.

One-Handed Dinner

An awesome activity that's not just fun, but also tests your ability to communicate clearly. The idea is to make dinner together, but each of you has to have one hand tied behind your back. During this exercise, you'll have to listen to instructions properly, help out awkwardly when two hands are needed, and just have some fun. It might create a mess, but cleaning it up together is another activity you can do together.

Create Lists Based on Names

More or less the same as the previous game that has you creating a list of all the things you love about a person, but a bit more interesting. Using the letters in your partner's name, come up with one word that describes them for every letter. You don't have to do this just once. Do it a few times and make it really tough.

The Miracle Question

Finally, the most revealing game of them all, and possibly the most dangerous. It's known by many names, but the basic premise is the same.

Once again, you take a piece of paper and answer one simple question: If you were to go to bed tonight, and a miracle transpired while you were asleep, what are the significant changes in your life you'd like to wake up to in the morning?

This will tell you a great deal about your partner. Perhaps they're still not ready to have a child, so they ask for a bigger house and a beautiful red Ferrari. Your answer will likely include waking up to the noise of a healthy baby in a beautifully built nursery, which is why you should proceed with caution with this exercise.

When Should I Try Therapy?

Good question. There's absolutely nothing wrong with therapy, except the stigma attached to it. It's more acceptable now than ever before, but some people still have strong feelings against it. Males especially have a tough time accepting the fact that they'll have to discuss their relationship in front of a complete stranger.

While I'm trying my best to give advice for every relationship scenario via clear communications, there are certain instances where you should seek professional advice. Just as I spent four years obtaining a degree in communications, these folks spent more time than that getting to know the human mind. It's also the reason why I only used verified doctors for important references in this book.

The signs that it's time to seek couples counseling are quite clear, with the first being having the same fight over and over with no conclusion. These fights tend to be about big life moments, finance, or when trust has been broken in some big way. Because the consequences of whatever action are so significant, neither party is willing to budge on their point of view. In that case, it's worth investing in an objective outsider to help you communicate your way through the problem.

The low self-confidence discussed earlier in this chapter can also manifest as full-blown depression, if not properly treated. When you start noticing that your partner is expressing nothing but apathy, or any of the other signs of depression (increase in fatigue, anxiety, weight loss) means it's time to seek professional help. Not only will he/she get the real help they deserve, but you'll be there with them, learning how you can support them.

Serious sex life issues are also a cause for concern. While I discussed the changes you can attempt earlier, you might want to seek professional help if you've already found yourself close to cheating. Some people simply can't get over the embarrassment of talking about it and need that extra help to get the conversation flowing.

We rely on our partners for emotional support, but when they fail us we seek it elsewhere. This is also a good cause to go see a therapist. On the topic of emotional support, it's worth mentioning serious loss in the family. When you lose a child, for example, you're going to need professional help.

The final reason to go is if your partner asks you to do it. Don't take this as a negative sign, in fact, is something to be thankful for. It's a clear sign that they still think there's something worth saving, and you owe it to them even if it makes you uncomfortable.

Chapter 7:

Conflict Resolution

Conflict is an inevitable and normal part of any healthy relationship. By now you've learned that it's perfectly fine to express your views, and at some point, these views will upset your partner.

These conflicts between you and your partner will range from big to small. You might argue over whether you want to go out on Saturday night, or a medium-sized argument about where to spend Christmas, all the way to the larger arguments that involve giving up jobs, moving, and buying a new property. And yes, we'll also be covering cheating, but since that's quite a big problem, we'll dedicate a segment just to that.

For now, here are some tips on how to handle conflict in a healthy way.

The Everyday Conflict

These are the small to medium-sized conflicts that we occasionally face. Dr. Gwendolyn Seidman offers sage advice in her piece, *10 Tips for Solving Relationship Conflicts* (Seidman, 2017).

The first piece of advice is to be direct. Throughout this book, we've seen various examples of mistakes people make, like not being honest about their feelings, or being passive-aggressive. By not being direct about what irks you, you're not giving your partner much to work with. You're essentially forcing them to play a guessing game, with no idea how to respond. All this does is waste time, and it adds to the anger. Be direct, tell them what the problem is, and take it from there.

The next step is to tell them what the problem is, without blaming them directly. Laying the blame at someone's feet from the very start creates unnecessary hostility. This all boils down to how you phrase the problem. Let's say the argument is about where to spend Christmas. A bad way to phrase it would be, "you never want to spend any time with my parents." This immediately blames the other person, and it's a statement that's not entirely true, especially if this person is more than happy to spend time with your parents. Rather say something along the lines of, "I feel like I haven't seen my parents over the holidays in a while, and that makes me sad." This way you're not blaming your partner for the problem directly, but they still know exactly what the problem is.

While we're on the topic of language, remove the word "never" from your vocabulary. It says that you're completely unwilling to compromise, and since any good relationship is based on compromises, you'll never get anywhere with "never."

Remember to stick to one issue, so you can really hash it out properly. This goes hand-in-hand with listening properly. When you try and solve multiple problems in one go, it just doesn't work out. Not only does it have a negative effect on the listening process, but there will be an information overload as well. For the record, when you're resolving conflict, you should always employ the active listening techniques I wrote about earlier in the book.

From there on you have to work hard to refrain from those inherent automatic defenses we use. Such as objecting to what they have to say from the very beginning to respond to their complaint with a complaint of your own, even if it's not relevant. I'll use my own life as an example of how we did it wrong after having our first child. My wife would complain that she didn't have enough time to get to everything that needed to be done around the house. In my mind, how could she not? She has eight hours, and only a baby to take care of. Instead of hearing her out and trying to find a workable solution, I instead deflected and told her that she was expecting too much of me. I only really started changing my ways when I implemented the next step, which is to look at the situation from a different perspective.

Once I started looking at the problem from her side, I realized that raising a baby was hard work. I had to actively sit and place myself in her shoes to experience what she went through on a daily basis. From there it was easy for me to wake up an hour earlier to help her get things started. That already made a huge difference. I'd recommend looking at your relationship from your partner's perspective, even if there is no conflict to resolve. It's always valuable to know what they're going through, but you have to remember to be completely objective about it.

Avoid unnecessary tactics, such as name-calling, or aggressive non-verbal gestures. Sarcasm also doesn't help. Basically, avoid any tactic you used to use when you were a teenager. Responding to a complaint with "whatever" does absolutely nothing but elevate the anger.

Don't fight bad behavior with bad behavior. If your partner is spending too much time with his/her friends, rather confront him/her about it than doing the same. By choosing to match his/her behavior, you're simply dragging out the conflict, and with more time comes more resentment.

Finally, know when to take a break from fighting. If you find yourself resorting to any of the negative communication tactics we covered in this book, it's better to just walk away, and take a few minutes alone. I find that having a code word for this is very helpful. When my wife and I have been at it for a while, I simply call out "ice cream," and we'll table it for a while. We'll calmly eat a bowl of ice cream at home, or go out for a drive and get some. This usually gives us enough time to gather ourselves, so we can start the argument back up, but hopefully making more progress.

More Serious Conflict

Unfortunately, avoidance is much easier than any of the tactics above. Use it for long enough, and you'll inevitably end up living with a stranger who you resent for not doing more to save the relationship.

Couple that with the fact that divorces are so cheap these days, it's no wonder people often take the easy way out. I have multiple friends who are on their third marriage, and none of them have hit 40. While I don't like to judge, I can't help but think this is part of a larger problem. We don't want to fight for our relationships anymore.

If you're on the verge of leaving a long term partner, I urge you to at least try these strategies first before you do so. Please note that this portion still doesn't cover cheating.

Dr. Leon Seltzer offers advice for serious conflict in his piece, *6 Steps to Resolve Relationship Conflicts, Once and for All* (Seltzer, 2016.) These steps are quite radical, so prepare yourself for a tough time.

The first step is for each of you to create a hurt diary. You'll need a few days to do this, because you want to write down every moment that hurt you over the course of the relationship, or since the problems started. At the end of this, nothing should be left unsaid. These are all the feelings and arguments that pop up over and over, in other words, the disputes that are never fully resolved.

Jot them down, but also write down the emotion that you feel when you think back on that memory. Did you feel dismissed, ridiculed, weak, worthless, ashamed, rejected, or unloved? These feelings are very important because it's the feelings we hold onto, and not the moment itself. While you compile this diary, a lot of anger and frustration will emerge. At times you might even feel like starting a fight right then and there, but keep a lid on your emotions until you're both finished with this tough project.

Next, you need to start scheduling sessions with each other. There will be as many sessions as there are entries in the diaries. The entries won't be discussed all in one go, because it's simply too much pent-up emotion to solve in one day.

Every session will consist of one person sending a message, and one person receiving it. The messenger will describe the situation, as well as the emotions it brought up. I'll give you an example: "You really made me feel ashamed of myself when you told your entire family that I can't cook. I know it's a joke between us, but saying it in front of all those people made me feel ridiculed."

The other party, in this case the listener, is just there to listen. The idea is to create empathy, so don't dismiss their memory and their feelings as unjust or silly. Your job is not to defend yourself, but to try and feel how they felt at that moment. And to eventually realize how you contributed, whether you meant to or not. When you've done this, it's your turn to speak by validating their feelings.

Then you swap around and do the same thing but from different sides. The listener now takes an entry from his diary and reads it to the person that was previously the messenger. They have the same obligations mentioned above.

The next step is to apologize, but not because your mind is making you feel obligated. Apologize because you well and truly understand, and have empathy for the situation they were in, and the emotions they felt. Remember that this is a two-way street, so you'll get your turn to hear an apology as well.

By doing this over and over, you get rid of a pile of rubbish standing in your path to happiness. Think of all your emotional baggage as a wall, and every time you have one of these sessions, you chip away a small portion of it.

The final step is to ask your partner whether your apology or response to their grievance was good enough. When you simply repeat their own words back at them and don't use your own words to explain how you would have felt in that situation, they might not be inclined to believe you. The good news is that you're both exploring feelings together, and chances are most of these feelings will overlap. Perhaps the other party was also embarrassed in front of the family, which makes it easier to have empathy with the example I used earlier.

With the serious conflict dealt with, we can move on to one of the biggest sins you can commit in a relationship - cheating.

How to Forgive a Cheater

You have one of two options when it comes to cheating. You can either kick your partner to the curb or choose to forgive them and try to rebuild a seriously damaged relationship. Here's how you do it.

The first step in this mess is to get it all out in the open, no matter how much it hurts. Tell your partner that you're willing to forgive them, but only if they're completely open about what happened, where it happened, why it happened, and how it happened.

This is the first step towards building trust again. Leaving out some of the details will leave lingering doubts, especially when it comes to the reason why he/she cheated. You'll always wonder if it's something you did or something they actively sought out because they were bored. One can't build a whole new foundation without fully understanding what happened.

At this point, you might want to start taking some of the blame, but don't do it. Even if their excuse is that they felt neglected by you. There are many other healthier ways you can communicate that you're feeling neglected. Jumping in the sack with someone else is not one of them. Don't feel guilty for a second.

Secondly, understand that you are taking a risk, and make sure your partner knows this. Instead of investing your time, moving on, and finding a new partner, you're choosing to invest in something that already has a history of failure. Take some comfort in the fact that nothing is hidden between you anymore. The worst has already happened, so the moment something happens that you don't like, or there is suspicious behavior, you don't have to feel like you're being overly-dramatic. You address any problems you have directly and openly.

The most immediate response will always be anger, which is perfectly understandable. But remember if you choose to take the path of forgiveness, you have some work to do. You'll want to take all that anger out on the cheater, but that's going to be counter-productive. Exploding like a bomb at every opportunity is not the answer, especially if there are kids involved. Rather deal with that rage in a healthy way. Talk to someone you trust, or if you don't feel like it's something you want to share, use some anger management tactics, like running, punching a bag at the gym. The best would be to go see a therapist because they are qualified to help you not only with your anger but through this whole process.

The next step is the hardest because it requires you to forgive. Not forget, mind you. Just forgiveness is the first real step towards recovery.

Allow me to explain why. At no point do you have to forget what your partner did, nor do you have to give them your trust back yet. But instead of picking a fight, constantly throwing it in their face, or bringing it up in conversation, making sarcastic remarks about it, or in any way reminding them of what they did, why not put that energy to good use. Channel all that energy into fixing the situation, and give your partner the opportunity to be better.

Finally, you need to give each other space. You won't be intimate for some time to come, and you need time alone to process. In a perfect scenario, the cheating partner would move out for a while, almost as if you're rewinding the relationship back to the dating phase. Explain the situation to the cheating partner clearly. You may have forgiven them, but earning that trust back is going to take some time. And in order to do that, you don't need to be constantly reminded of the source of your pain. Explain that it's just temporary, so there's no resentment from their side, even though they don't really have a strong case for feeling that way.

You'll know your relationship is fully restored once you can think of the other person without feeling anger or resentment. Once you can accept the fact that we all make mistakes, even though this is the biggest mistake you can make. Only then will you forgive fully, and not because your partner deserves it. You forgive because it's for you. You no longer want to live in the past with a cloud constantly hanging over the relationship.

You've both moved on, hopefully, busy growing a better, stronger relationship.

How to End It

Some relationships are beyond saving, and breaking up is just a natural result. That's why I included it in this book as well. While reading it, you may have recognized that you are currently in a toxic relationship and that you'd rather end it. You'd rather put what you learned in this book to work in your next relationship. That's perfectly fine. It's your life, after all.

Breaking up is hard. Most of us tend to have sympathy for the person being broken up with, but it's a sad affair for both parties involved. Let's not forget that at some point this couple was happy, and they likely have many happy memories to look back on. That's worth keeping in mind. Don't look at a breakup as an opportunity to harm your partner, but rather as an opportunity to part ways in a way that's sad at first, but not so sad that it overshadows all the good times you had. That way you can always look back at the relationship fondly, and even use the lessons you learned from it when you find a new partner. But you can only break up in this way if you communicate efficiently. No ghosting, letting them know that you're over it via a text message or changing your relationship status on Facebook.

You'll experience a lot of guilt during this period, and perhaps even pressure from friends and family who don't want you to do it. While guilt is a difficult emotion to get rid of, take some comfort in the fact that you're doing it not just for yourself, but for the other person as well. You don't want to be with them anymore, and while they don't realize it yet, one day they'll understand that nobody wants to be with a person who doesn't really want to be with them. A relationship built on a sense of obligation is doomed to be unhappy.

The first step is to not avoid pulling the band-aid off. Do it as soon as you've made the decision, and do the other person the courtesy of doing it in person. Doing it via text may be the easy way out, but you only leave the other person confused and hurt. When you break up with someone, they at least deserve a full explanation as to why you chose to do it. That can only be done in person.

When you do it, be honest about your feelings, and be very clear about the reason you're breaking it off. It's a respectful thing to do, and it helps them get closure. There is a caveat here, however. You should be honest, but don't cross a line and be brutally honest. One of the reasons you may be leaving your partner is because you don't feel sexually satisfied. Keep in mind that not all people are compatible sexually and that there's no need to say something along the lines of "you're just not any good at sex." A statement like that can have lasting damage on the person you're leaving behind. Their self-esteem will take a knock, and as we've seen before in this book, self-esteem is a big issue. Don't set them up for failure in their next relationship by being brutally honest.

As the person doing the breaking up, you carry the responsibility of your decision. This means you have to answer any questions your partner may have.

Whatever you do, make sure that it's clear that the relationship is over. After the breaking up part is done, keep your distance for a while to ensure that a new routine is established, and you not being in their life is part of their new normal.

There are also things you should avoid. You never break up in public, and you never break the person down. It's also imperative that you don't offer any kind of false hope by saying that you can still be friends, or by having breakup sex. All of these things send a mixed message, which is exactly what you don't want.

Communicating After the Relationship Ends

The segment above is the best-case scenario for breaking things off, but I mentioned kids at one point for one very good reason. In certain cases, it's just not possible to make a clean break from an ex-partner, and having to raise a child between you isn't the only example. It's also difficult to avoid someone if you work in the same industry, or if your families are close friends. There are various examples where you just have to make peace with the fact that you're going to be seeing your ex on a regular basis. So, how does that kind of communication between you work?

The go-to emotion might still be anger, but there are other factors to consider. If you choose to communicate in a manner that is rude, what will the effect be on your kids? If it's work-related, you'll be creating a hostile working environment. If your families were friends long before you got together, you might even create a choosing sides situation. That's extremely unfair, given that their relationship existed long before yours did.

I'd suggest a face-to-face conversation in a neutral setting. Hopefully, the relationship ended amicably enough for you to have a civil discussion. Take the time to just lay some basic ground rules, the main one being that you'll do your utmost not to make it uncomfortable for your mutual coworkers, friends, family, or kids.

The rules are entirely up to you, but I do have some tips that might help things run a bit smoother.

The first piece of advice is the criteria you should use when contacting your ex. Do you have a good reason, or are you just making conversation? I mention it because it's an easy trap to fall into. When we're feeling vulnerable, we crave something familiar and soothing. Before you know it, you're calling your ex or sending them a text just to make conversation. Already you're treading on dangerous territory, especially if kids are involved, and especially if you're the one who did the breaking up. Starting a casual conversation about something irrelevant only creates false hope. And while your moment of vulnerability might be fleeting, your ex's renewed hope will definitely not be.

There are much better ways to pass this fleeting moment of depression. Instead of connecting with your ex, rather connect with a friend that you lost touch with.

Valid reasons to talk to your ex include any arrangements you need to make with regards to the kids and obviously emergency situations. When you need advice from the other parent, it's also perfectly fine to ask for help. When it comes to mutual friends and family, just keep it to small talk. Your friends will probably initially know not to invite you to the same events, but as time passes you'll be able to converse like old friends. Even if the rage still lingers after a few years, be the better person and act civil. Your friends and family will respect you for it.

Talking to them for the first time post-breakup might seem daunting, but you likely have a few years' worth of first-hand experience in dealing with this person and don't be afraid to use that knowledge to your advantage. Ask them how their hobby is going, break the ice, and then get to the real reason you're phoning.

Topics to avoid include bringing up the reasons you broke up, and how you've changed since then. Don't play the comparison game, even though you really want to prove that you ended up in a better place. Your new partner may be an absolute knockout that makes millions per year, but it's poor form to bring that up in conversation.

Conclusion

Proper communication is hard, and relationships are even harder. But by improving one, we can easily improve the other.

The trouble with communication is that there is no one-size-fits-all solution. We communicate according to our personalities, and there are just so many things that a personality is made up of. It depends on your cultural background, your gender, the way you were raised, and how quickly you lose your temper. And that's just scratching the surface.

We're also afraid to speak up or express ourselves in a non-verbal way. Even the most confident person will not speak up out of fear of being dismissed or ridiculed. We project our own fears onto those around us.

So we stay quiet until we eventually reach a boiling point. And by then it's too late for a decent discussion. A highly emotional person letting off steam will almost always use hurtful tactics, such as screaming, name-calling, and sarcasm.

This has to change. The fear has to go away, and all need to do in order for that to happen is to ask yourself, what's the worst that could possibly happen? Best case scenario, you end up having a proper heart-to-heart with your partner, and you end up closer as a result. Worst case scenario you have a fight, which, as we've seen, is also just another cog in the machine. At least during a fight grievances get aired. Keeping quiet, and attempting to be content while you're secretly unhappy is unfair to you, and your partner.

You have an opportunity to change the way you communicate by leading by example. Rather than reading this book, and handing it over to your partner to read, implement these changes in your life, and form new habits. I guarantee your partner will pick up on it, and respond to the changes positively.

It's even better if you have kids in the house because they'll learn proper communication techniques from a young age via the example you set. Hopefully, the next generation won't have to turn to books like this to learn how to communicate their feelings.

I hate to break things up into gender, but there are big differences in the way we communicate. I can only speak from my own experiences as a man married to a woman, but I've spoken to enough people and witnessed enough arguments in my time to make some reasonable conclusions.

As men, we have a generally negative attitude towards talking unnecessarily. We see it only as a function that has to have a clear purpose. Women, on the other hand, don't see it as talking. They see it as sharing. There's also a decent helping of toxic masculinity involved. Talking about your feelings is not regarded as manly, whatever that means. To me, there's nothing more manly than being vulnerable. It shows that you actually have nothing to prove to anyone, which is the highest level of self-confidence you can achieve.

There's also a big difference in the amount we talk. Given that men want to use talking as effectively as possible, they don't say much. Women, on the other hand, paint an elaborate picture using words. I love asking my wife how her day was. Instead of just telling me that a new actor started, she'll give me their entire life story.

Women are more effective listeners than men are. They're much better at the active listening thing, while men assume every act of communication is a search for advice. As you read earlier in this book, sometimes you just need somebody to listen, to understand, and to have empathy. On that exact same topic, when a woman tells you about her problems, she's not actually asking you to fix them for her. Nine times out of ten, she just wants a set of ears to listen. She's a big girl, she has the ability to fix her own problems at work, or wherever they may be. Unless she actually asks you to get involved, don't just assume that you need to go fix whatever problem on her behalf.

Men, on the other hand, tend to withdraw when something is wrong. Women are just as inclined to want to fix problems on our behalf, which we tend to take the wrong way. The result is usually about of the silent treatment, which is now so famous that it has its own meme. You know the one where a couple is lying in bed, and she's convinced he's thinking about another woman when he's actually just wondering why Tony Stark never made an Iron Man suit for Captain America.

I have to say that the 2020 pandemic did some good when it comes to communication problems in general.

People joked about divorce rates skyrocketing, but I actually think it had the opposite effect. Perhaps what some people needed was to be locked in with their significant other, with no place to escape to. I'm sure there were some fights, and I can only hope that they ended well. I know it did my relationship a world of good. Not only did I get to spend so much time just talking to my wife, but with my kids as well. I've never felt more in harmony with my wife than I do at this point.

I also think the pandemic caused a shift in the way we experience shame. Before this chaotic occurrence, losing a job due to budget cuts was something to be ashamed of. You didn't want others to know. It also wasn't socially acceptable to feel lonely, or depressed. Those were feelings you buried deep down and never spoke about. But this pandemic brought on a shift. Because so many people lost their jobs, the shame is gone. We all know at least one person that was affected by it, and we talk about it openly and with empathy. For the first time ever, it's also okay to say that you're not okay. I had friends phone me up, just to chat. And for the most part, they admitted that they were lonely. I've known these men for more than half my life, and that's never happened before.

In closing, I'd like to reinforce what I said near the beginning of this book. If you look back on it now, I think you'll agree with me that the biggest communication problem we have is that we don't listen anymore.

The main problem is the way information is distributed these days. There's simply too much of it and not enough time to go through all of it. Instead of reading one news article properly, we read five headlines and think we know what happened. The political turmoil doesn't help either, with neither side giving the other the decency of listening. If we look at Maslow's hierarchy of needs, we notice that there's nothing on there that's political, or cultural for that matter. It's all basic human needs, and we all have that in common. One of those needs is being heard, and if we all just stand back for a second and think about it properly, we'd realize how much further we'd get just by listening.

I left the personality traits that stand between you and listening properly for last, because that's what I want to leave you with. Do some introspection, and if you only take one lesson from this book, let it be that you need to listen more and not let these things get in the way.

The first is our desire to communicate what we know because we want to come across as knowledgeable and interesting. That's why you're not listening when the other person speaks because you're already formulating a response that will make you sound smart. There's no shame in listening, taking a moment to think, and then responding. You'll actually be setting a good example, and people will like talking to you more. Like I said above, one of our basic needs is to be heard, so hear people out.

Also, consider your own cultural background when talking to people. It's so easy to make assumptions about other people because you assume that they had the same background as you. Let me give you a simple example. Let's say you're sitting with a group of friends, and you're talking about your younger years. You'll complain about how embarrassing it was to kiss your mother in front of the school when she dropped you off. Consider for a moment that other people might not have had a similar experience. Perhaps their parents were too poor for a car, so they had to walk. They'd have only been too happy for that kiss. It doesn't invalidate your feelings, but keep in mind that not every person you come across has the same background as you.

Then we have ego and selfishness. You may think you're the smartest person in the room, but I'll let you in on a little secret: The actual smartest person in the room never thinks they are. The smartest person in the room is the one who doesn't think they are. They're usually the person that listens, just so they can learn more. Never let your ego stand in the way of learning something new.

When it comes to selfishness, we all know that one person who has to make everything about them. You know the one. You'll be telling a story about your holiday to Thailand, and they'll interrupt you to tell you all about their time in Vietnam. If your grandma is sick, theirs is sicker. These people have a constant craving for attention, and it most likely stems from a lack of self-esteem. Use the methods in this book to help them out with that.

You have the power to communicate more effectively with your partner. All you need to do is take that first step, so here's what I want you to do.

Tonight, when they get home, ask them how their day was, and go above and beyond the usual small talk. Then just sit back, listen, and take it from there.

References

Abrams, A. (2017, March 27). *8 Steps to Improving Your Self-Esteem.* Psychology Today. https://www.psychologytoday.com/za/blog/nurturing-self-compassion/201703/8-steps-improving-your-self-esteem

Boyes, A. (2015, December 29). *7 Ways to Give Your Partner a Boost.* Psychology Today. https://www.psychologytoday.com/us/blog/in-practice/201512/7-ways-give-your-partner-boost

Cloé Madanes. (2013). *Relationship breakthrough : how to create outstanding relationships in every area of your life.* Rodale. (Original work published 2020)

Definition of COMMUNICATION. (2019). Merriam-Webster.com. https://www.merriam-webster.com/dictionary/communication

Definition of EMPATHY. (n.d.). Www.Merriam-Webster.com. Retrieved November 9, 2020, from https://www.merriam-webster.com/dictionary/empathy#note-1

Goldsmith, B. (2013, March 4). *10 Things Your Relationship Needs to Thrive.* Psychology Today. https://www.psychologytoday.com/za/blog/emotional-fitness/201303/10-things-your-relationship-needs-thrive

Graff, M. (2018, February 22). *Does Sexting Have Benefits for Your Relationship?* Psychology Today. https://www.psychologytoday.com/za/blog/love-digitally/201802/does-sexting-have-benefits-your-relationship#:~:text=In%20terms%20of%20the%20positive

how-to-be-an-effective-communicator-in-7-easy-steps. (n.d.). Www.Waldenu.Edu. Retrieved November 22, 2020, from https://www.waldenu.edu/programs/communication/resource/how-to-be-an-effective-communicator-in-7-easy-steps

Maslow, A. (1943). *A theory of human motivation.* Psycnet.Apa.org. https://psycnet.apa.org/record/1943-03751-001

Milenkovic, J. (2020, February 11). *How Much Time Does the Average Person Spend on Their Phone?* KommandoTech. https://kommandotech.com/statistics/how-much-time-does-the-average-person-spend-on-their-phone/

Pietrzak, M. (2019, January 11). *12 Steps to Breaking Smartphone Addiction.* SUCCESS. https://www.success.com/12-steps-to-breaking-smartphone-addiction/

Ronald E, R. (2011, August 3). *Are You Empathic? 3 Types of Empathy and What They Mean.* Psychology Today.

https://www.psychologytoday.com/us/blog/c
utting-edge-leadership/201108/are-you-
empathic-3-types-empathy-and-what-they-mean

Schwartz, A. B. (2015, May 6). *The Infamous "War of the Worlds" Radio Broadcast Was a Magnificent Fluke.* Smithsonian   Magazine. https://www.smithsonianmag.com/history/inf amous-war-worlds-radio-broadcast-was-magnificent-fluke-180955180/#:~:text=Broadcast%20Hysteria% 3A%20Orson%20Welles

Seidman, G. (2017, April 17). *10 Tips for Solving Relationship Conflicts.* Psychology Today. https://www.psychologytoday.com/za/blog/cl ose-encounters/201704/10-tips-solving-relationship-conflicts

Seltzer, L. (2016, November 16). *6 Steps to Resolve Relationship Conflicts, Once and for All.* Psychology Today. https://www.psychologytoday.com/za/blog/ev olution-the-self/201610/6-steps-resolve-relationship-conflicts-once-and-all

Whitbourne, S. K. (2014, January 14). *The 9 Most Common Relationship Mistakes.* Psychology Today. https://www.psychologytoday.com/za/blog/fu lfillment-any-age/201401/the-9-most-common-relationship-mistakes

www.ingramcontent.com/pod-product-compliance
Lightning Source LLC
Chambersburg PA
CBHW070115030426
42335CB00016B/2157